A Guide to
BIRDWATCHING
in the
THE LAKE DISTRICT
and the
COAST OF CUMBRIA

by
David Watson

First published in 2011 by
Photoprint Scotland

© David & Rosemary Watson
watson.dr@btinternet.com

ISBN 978-0-9559438-8-1

Photography by David & Rosemary Watson
For additional photographs, see Acknowledgements, page 112
Graphics and design by Rosemary Watson

Printed and bound by MLG, Glasgow

CONTENTS

INTRODUCTION

At the time when children were allowed out to roam without fear, Grune Point and the landward edge of Skinburness Marsh was my playground. We certainly had a wide knowledge of birds and knew the call of the Shelducks in the creeks and the rasping voice of the Corncrake in the hay meadows, never thinking that it might not be there for ever.

I was born in Silloth on the Solway coast and spent my early childhood at Pond Cottage, Skinburness, overlooking the marshes. After Nelson Thomlinson Grammar School in Wigton, followed by university in Bristol reading Geography , I set off to Africa, especially inspired by Bernhard Grzimek's book on the great migrations, "Serengeti Shall Not Die".

Many years later, in the 1990s, my wife Rosemary and I, living in Kenya, were privileged to get involved in mapping national parks and reserves, which also involved wildlife photography and the writing of guides. Before we finally settled again in Scotland, we had mapped, photographed and written about world-known sites such as Masai Mara, Serengeti, Ngorongoro Crater, Tsavo, Amboseli and Lewa, as well as producing books on Tanzania and Kenya.

"A Guide to Birdwatching in the Lake District" is our fifth Simple Guide on the Lake District, but our first on wildlife-watching since we returned from Africa. Preparing for it has been a great pleasure, with birdwatching experiences every bit as exciting and amazing as those for which we travelled half way round the world.

I hope this book, telling you where you can watch birds in the Lake District and the coast of Cumbria, will provide a catalyst for many to begin to appreciate the wildlife of this incredible little corner of the world.

David Watson

Skinburness and the edge of the marsh

The book is in two parts. The first identifies and describes the wide range of habitats found in the Lake District and the areas close by, and of a "stretched" coast of Cumbria, extending from Caerlaverock, on the north Solway coast, down to Leighton Moss, which is in north Lancashire. Each habitat is described in detail, together with the most likely bird species one might find there. The habitat colour-coding is carried through to the second section.

Part 2 identifies about 40 of the best places to watch birds. Each is described with a selection of classified information on its designation, management, disabled access, a "How to get there" box, and a sketch map to show location, and sometimes a bit more detail. For each site, the special points of interest are explained.

Waders in the Duddon estuary

Rhythms of birdwatching

Successful birdwatching requires us to be in tune with the rhythms of nature, of which there are several.

Most obvious is the rhythm of the seasons, affecting annual migrations, and the time to mate and nest. Many of Britain's birds are only here for a season. Some, like Barnacle geese, come for the winter, to escape from the cold of the Arctic. Others, such as Swallows, come for the summer to nest, at the time when there is enough food about for their young.

Some birds follow a daily rhythm, spending the day in one habitat, and the night in another. Pinkfoot geese need the security of a night-time roost on the sea, but fly back inland to feed at dawn.

Wading birds are controlled by the tides. They can only access the rich inter-tidal mudflats when the tide is out, and so, as the tide comes in, they feed further and further up the beach until, eventually, they are forced to roost on the adjacent land. And as the time of the tides advances by approximately an hour each day, birds which feed on the mudflats must also alter their lunchtime every day.

Successful birdwatching needs to follow the same rhythms.

Habitats & Species

Lakes, Rivers & Wetlands

The Essentials: Lakes are highly variable in their attraction for birds. Some are nutrient-rich and bird friendly. Others are impoverished, with fewer birds. Some lakes are deep whereas others have shallows suitable for dabbling ducks. They are important as a winter refuge for seabirds, waders and wildfowl. There are important wetlands at the ends of some lakes.

The Lake District has almost 20 lakes, depending on which you include, and apart from the high fells, this is the archetypal landscape which gives the region its name.

The pattern resembles the spokes of a wheel, with the centre between Scafell and Helvellyn. But a habitat for bird life, the lakes vary according to their geology, the nature of the floor of the lake, and the stage which has been reached in the inevitable infilling of the lake basin. They are amongst the most transient features in the landscape, and in the 10,000 or so years since the last glaciation some lakes, such as Derwentwater and Bassenthwaite are already well on the way to being filled i with the sediment which provides a rich habitat for birds. But others such as Wastwater are deep and rocky, and create a more impoverished bird habitat.

How are different parts of the habitat used by different birds?

Fish eaters
Fish eating birds including Ospreys, Cormorants, Red-breasted Merganser and Goosander eat quite large fish. Little grebes, Great-crested grebes and Grey herons tend to eat smaller fish.

Male Osprey

Brotherswater

Nutrient rich lakes, with lots of bird life include Derwentwater, Bassenthwaite, Esthwaite, Ullswater, Windermere and Brotherswater.

Wastwater

Nutrient poor lakes, with fewer birds include Wastwater, Buttermere and Ennerdale Water.

Invertebrates and Plant Eaters
Some species, such as Tufted ducks, eat invertebrates, whereas Pochard search out a range of aquatic plants.
Dabblers
The so-called "dabbling ducks", such as Mallard and Teal, are frequently seen up-ended in shallow water, searching out all sorts of food items, ranging from seeds and aquatic plants, to larvae, worms, snails and frogs.

Many birds simply use the lakes as a roost, feeding on nearby marshy fields during the day and returning to the safety of the lakes at night.
Some seabirds, such as a range of divers, use the lakes as a refuge when the conditions at sea are especially severe in the winter.
In summer the air above the water is usually full of insects, and Swifts, Swallows and Martins all use the edge of the lakes as a favoured feeding ground.

Opposite: Corner of Derwentwater

Wetlands at the head of the lakes

As lakes are filled in, and in some cases split in two, they create wetlands, at the head of the lake and in some cases around the edges, often with reedbeds, sedge, alder and willow. Largest of these is Braithwaite Bog at the head of Bassenthwaite, but there are also wetlands between Grange and Derwentwater, and at the southern ends of both Windermere and Coniston, and around numerous lowland tarns.

Such wetlands are an especially attractive habitat for a range of birds, including Yellow Wagtail, Snipe, Sedge and Grasshopper Warblers.

Wetlands of Esthwaite

Wetlands of Derwentwater at Lodore

Braithwaite Bog

Above left: Pair of well-concealed Snipe
Left: Pied Wagtail

Resident Birds
Canada goose
Coot
Dipper
Dunlin
Goosander
Grey heron
Greylag goose
Grey wagtail
Great-crested grebe
Kingfisher
Lapwing
Little grebe
Mallard
Moorhen
Oystercatcher
Pied wagtail
Pochard
Red-breasted merganser
Redshank
Reed bunting
Teal
Tufted duck

Winter Visitors
Bewick swan
Black-necked grebe
Black-throated diver
Cormorant
Dunlin
Goldeneye
Great northern diver
Greylag goose
Gulls of wide variety
Pochard
Red-throated diver
Slavonian grebe
Teal
Tufted duck
Whooper swan
Wigeon

Summer Visitors
Black-headed gulls
Great black-backed gulls
Herring gulls
House martins
Lesser blackbacked gulls
Osprey
Sedge warblers
Sand martin
Swallow
Swift

Fells
& Crags

The Essentials: Lakeland fells give an impoverished and deforested landscape; acid grassland and bracken; poor for birds, though some specialist species like the habitat. Crags are highly variable cliffs and rock outcrops, most pronounced in central Lakeland. Inaccessibility to sheep makes it one of the best places for remnants of original woodland and shrub vegetation, therefore a much richer bird habitat than the fellsides.

Most of the Lake District is now made up of bare hills, mainly covered in acid grassland and bracken. But immediately after the last ice age, about 10,000 years ago, trees and shrubs extended up the hills to about 500 metres. Most of the trees, such as oak, birch and elm, together with low-growing species such as hazel and holly, had their maximum between 6,000 and 10,000 years ago, but since then, for various reasons, there has been a general retreat of trees and shrubs to gills, ravines, inaccessible crags and a few favoured lower dales.

Undoubtedly some of this is due to a change in the climate which occurred about 5,000 years ago, and from the Neolithic time onwards, when agriculture began, there has been a gradual but relentless clearing of the Cumbrian forest. However, most serious for the demise of the Lakeland upland habitat was the arrival of sheep farming as the basic agricultural system. More than any other domestic animals, perhaps with the exception of goats, sheep reduce the ability of woodland to regenerate, so producing the Lake District landscape we see today.

Wheatear

Resident Birds

Buzzard	Pied wagtail
Fieldfare	Raven
Golden eagle	Reed bunting
Jackdaw	Stonechat
Kestrel	Wren
Meadow pipit	Yellowhammer
Peregrine	

(In reality many will seasonally
"migrate" up and down the fells)

Summer Visitors

Cuckoo
Dotterel
Ring ouzel
Wheatear
Whinchat

Winter Visitors

Snow bunting
Twite

Twite

Kestrel

Buzzard

Until recently, the upper Haweswater valley enjoyed England's only pair of breeding golden eagles. However, at the time of writing there is no female, though the male still displays in the spring, in the hope of attracting a mate.

Look out also for a few bracken nesters, such as reed buntings and yellowhammers.

There is one bird which you find everywhere, from the cliffs at St Bees, to high up on the Cumbrian fells, the wren, probably Britain's most prolific bird. Many very high altitude Lakeland crags have wrens nesting on them.

During the winter, when most birds have at least descended to the lowlands, you may be lucky enough to encounter visitors from Iceland, snow buntings.

From the perspective of the birdwatcher the Lakeland fells are a relatively impoverished habitat. However, there are some positives. Sheep do provide dead animals for a range of carrion eaters such as Ravens, Buzzards and very occasional Golden eagles. Red kites have also colonized many sheep pastures in Scotland, and in 2010 were re-introduced to Grizedale Forest.

The ubiquitous dry-stone walls, which are iconic to Lakeland also provide important benefits, being used as nesting sites for quite a range of birds, including Ring ouzel, Peregrine, Raven, Kestrel, Jackdaw, Buzzard and Wheatear.

Tarns and Streams

The Essentials: Refers to mountain tarns and upland streams. A relatively poor, unproductive habitat, which improves the lower the altitude. Severe winters generally cause breeding species to migrate to the coast or the lowlands after nesting.

The word "tarn" means a small lake or large pond, usually, though not always, in the mountains. Because of their altitude and severe winter conditions, Lakeland hill tarns are generally not rich in aquatic life, and where there are birds, the shortage of food usually means they have a larger territory than further downstream. This is true of Dippers and Pied wagtails, which are commonly seen.

Some species, such as Goosander and Snipe use this habitat for nesting, but retreat to the lowlands and the coast at the end of the summer. One should be aware that the higher tarns are a fairly unproductive environment for the birdwatcher, whereas things improve with tarns of lower altitude.

Breeding birds on mountain tarns or in the vicinity

Black-headed gull
Common sandpiper
Coot
Dipper
Grey heron
Grey wagtail
Goosander
Pied wagtail
Snipe

Winter visitors
Bewick swan
Goldeneye
Pochard
Whooper swan

Whooper swan

Goldeneye

Grey heron

Dippers

Moorland

The Essentials: Heather, bilberry, bracken and blanket bog, mostly disappeared from the Lake District. The best areas of moorland are in the north Pennines and provide important habitat for some birds such as Red and Black grouse.

Never grazed by sheep   Heavily grazed by sheep in the past

The term "moorland" refers mainly to upland covered in heather (calluna vulgaris), traditionally known in the Lake District as "ling", together with various species of erica, bilberry, bracken and blanket bog, usually with cotton grass. If we go by the evidence of place names including the word "ling", moorland was originally much more widespread than it is today. But intensive grazing of sheep over the last 200 years put paid to that, and today Lakeland heather moorland is confined to only a few places such as the northern slopes of Skiddaw, the vicinity of Devoke Water, and around inaccessible crags and ravines. The greatest expanses of moorland are to the east, on the northern Pennines, and so we will stretch our definition of the "Lake District", as we will with a few other habitats, to include Geltsdale, the huge reserve southeast of Brampton, a prime moorland site, owned by the RSPB.

Black grouse

Moorland gives food and security during breeding to the archetypal Red grouse, and to the spectacular, but much threatened Black grouse. Wrens are everywhere, and Peregrines, Merlins and Hen harriers hunt residents and summer breeders alike. Some species, such as the Snipe and Golden plover breed in the moorland, but descend to the Solway Plains to escape the harshness of the winter.

Residents

(S) *British birds which winter in the Solway lowlands*
Barn owl
Black grouse (Black cock)
Buzzard
Dipper
Golden plover (S)
Hen harrier
Meadow pipit (S)
Merlin
Peregrine
Raven
Red grouse
Redshank (S)
Short-eared owl
Stonechat (S)
Twite
Wren

Winter visitors

Fieldfare
Redwing
Teal

Summer visitors

Curlew
Dunlin
Golden plover
Lapwing
Ring ouzel
Skylark
Snipe
Swallow
Wheatear
Whinchat

Red grouse

Barn owl

Lapwing

Heather moorland

Deciduous Woodland

Essentials: Original habitat of most of Lakeland to about 500 metres, now restricted to crags, ravines and a few protected areas such as Borrowdale, south of Grange. Originally there was a wider range of tree species. Now oak predominates, providing a rich habitat for birds, especially where there is a thriving under-storey of shrubs such as hazel and holly.

During the first few millennia after the final retreat of the glaciers, Cumbria enjoyed a rich woodland flora. Pollen evidence on the floor of mountain tarns tells us that oak, elm, hazel and juniper were found 500 metres up the fellside. However, over the intervening years, as a result of a combination of changing climate, together with the influence of man, woodland has gradually retreated down the mountainside, and into the gills or on to inaccessible crags. The adoption of sheep grazing over the last few hundred years as the basic agricultural activity, completed the process of general woodland clearance.

Today, although the fells are bare of trees, a few favoured woodland habitats remain, especially in Borrowdale south of the village of Grange, where most of the woods are owned by the National Trust. There are also smaller pockets of deciduous woodland in many valleys, including Buttermere, Loweswater and in Grizedale, between Windermere and Coniston. Sessile oak, formerly used for coppicing, is common, together with wych elm, ash, alder and hazel. Some areas, such as the south-eastern shore of Ullswater, have downy birch with a shrub layer of juniper and holly.

Brambling

Oak trees especially create a rich habitat for birds, harbouring over 300 varieties of insects. The trees are also very long-lived, and as they age they form all sorts of holes and hollows which provide nesting sites for birds. When oak trees die they become home to over 200 varieties of fungi.

Treecreeper

Deciduous woodland on limestone provides an especially rich and different habitat, for example at Whitbarrow in southern Lakeland. Here ash predominates over oak, and there is a rich hazel understorey, together with yew and a wide variety of tree and shrub species. Generally limestone provides a richer habitat than more acid rocks.

Tawny owl

Residents	Treecreeper
Blue tit	Woodcock
Buzzard	Wren
Chaffinch	**Summer visitors**
Coal tit	Garden warbler
Great spotted woodpecker	Pied flycatcher
Great tit	Redstart
Hawfinch	Tree pipit
Long-tailed tit	Whitethroat
Lesser spotted woodpecker	Willow warbler
Marsh tit	Wood warbler
Nuthatch	**Winter visitors**
Sparrowhawk	Redpoll
Tawny owl	Siskin

Whitbarrow

Coniferous Woodland

Essentials: A 20th century phenomenon in Lakeland, with the degree of attraction of conifers to birds varying with the age of the plantation. From initial planting to mature trees, bird species change from those choosing the open fields and fells, to a few which are truly "conifer specialists".

Apart from the juniper, evergreen or coniferous woodland is non-native to Cumbria, though great swathes now occupy the fellsides, especially around Bassenthwaite, Grizedale and in Ennerdale.

The introduction of conifers totally changes the habitat, removing a wide range of food sources, but introducing others. As coniferous plantations become established, so the habitat gradually changes over a period of about 15 years, producing different ranges of bird species at different times.

In the early years of a plantation the original birds of the open fell or of the woodland edge will still be there, but their population will gradually decrease. These include Short-eared owls, Hen harriers, Skylarks and Meadow pipits. Some birds such as Ravens and Merlins will eventually be totally displaced.

From 15 years onwards, as the canopy of conifers becomes complete, one can identify a different population of "woodland" birds, including Chaffinches, Gold crest, Treecreepers, Coal tits, Sparrowhawks and Woodcock.

A few birds are conifer specialists. One such is the Crossbill, which is able to remove seeds from cones, apparently of any age, but with a greater preference for mature cones.

Red grouse

Siskin

Chaffinch

Residents	
Chaffinch	Wheatear
Coal tit	Woodcock
Crossbill (also winter migrants)	Woodpigeon
	Wren
Dunnock	
Goldcrest	**Winter visitors**
Goshawk	Crossbill
Hen harrier	Siskin
Meadow pipit	Short-eared owl
Robin	
Red grouse (forest edges)	**Summer visitors**
Short-eared owl (also some winter visitors)	Grasshopper warbler
	Nightjar
Sparrowhawk	Sedge warbler
Skylark	Whinchat
Treecreeper	Whitethroat
	Willow warbler

Short-eared owl

Estuaries & Salt Marshes

Essentials: Internationally important for overwintering waders and wildfowl. Large intertidal mudflats and shingle scars, with sea-washed salt marshes on the landward side. Huge numbers of many bird species.

The estuaries of the Cumbrian coast, associated mud-flats and adjacent salt-marshes, make up one of the richest bird habitats in the British Isles. There are two major areas, the first being the Solway in the north, comprising the combined mouths of the river Eden and the Border Esk, together with the area called Moricambe Bay, the estuary of the rivers Wampool and Waver. Secondly, in the south is the vast intertidal area of Morecambe Bay and the Duddon Estuary. These areas exhibit a variety of habitats, which together provide food for thousands of waders and wildfowl, especially those which arrive in Britain each autumn from the north and east to over-winter.

The major attraction for birds is the area of intertidal mudflats, exposed as the tide goes out, providing an enormous wealth of worms and crustaceans for a wide variety of waders. As the tides advance and retreat, twice every day, so the wading birds process up and down the beach. It is when the tide is at its highest that birdwatching is often at its best. Tide tables are available online or at almost all newsagents along the coast.

www.tidetimes.org.uk

Inland from the mudflats are extensive salt marshes, including Caerlaverock, Rockliffe, Drumburgh, Skinburness and those surrounding Moricambe Bay. Very few birds nest here due to frequent flooding, but the marshes are an integral link in the estuarine ecosystem, and many birds will move there to feed or to rest at high tide.

Out in the estuary are sand and shingle banks, frequently with mussel beds, locally known as "scars", eg Stenor Scar, off Grune Point. These provide another attractive habitat for waders. See maps for those which are most visible.

Numerous species migrate on a daily or tidal pattern between the estuaries and salt marshes, and the adjacent fields of the Solway Plain. The daily movements of over-wintering wildfowl are described in detail in part two of the book, suffice to say that huge flocks of Barnacle, Greylag and Pinkfoot geese will roost in the safety of the estuary, either on the water or on the mudflats, and then set off to inland feeding grounds at dawn.

Some species of gulls, especially Great black-backed, Lesser black-backed and Herring gulls feed on the mud-flats and fly inland at high tide, whereas others such as the Black-headed gull feed inland during the day, and return to the coast at night to roost.

Huge bird numbers also attract predators. Peregrines take mainly wading birds and small ducks, whereas Merlins concentrate on the smaller ground-nesting species such as Skylarks. Where there are fringing reedbeds on the landward side of the salt-marshes, for example at Leighton Moss, one finds Short-eared owls and Hen harriers.

In spite of its enormous importance for food, the estuarine habitat is relatively unimportant for breeding. However, shingle beds which are generally free from flooding, such as Grune Point or South Walney are important for some species of Tern, Oystercatchers and Ringed plovers, as well as other ground-nesting birds such as Meadow pipits and Skylarks.

Deep creek on Skinburness Marsh

Estuaries and Salt Marshes

Look out for the following birds

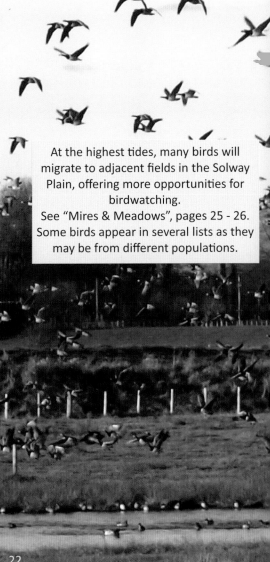

Residents

Cormorant	Merlin
Curlew	Moorhen
Dunlin	Oystercatcher
Eider duck	Peregrine
Herring gull	Redshank
Great black-backed gull	Reed bunting
	Ringed plover
Greylag goose	Shelduck
Grey wagtail	Short-eared owl
Lapwing	Skylark
Lesser black-backed gull	Snipe
	Stonechat
Mallard	Teal
Meadow pipit	Wigeon

At the highest tides, many birds will migrate to adjacent fields in the Solway Plain, offering more opportunities for birdwatching.
See "Mires & Meadows", pages 25 - 26.
Some birds appear in several lists as they may be from different populations.

Winter Visitors

Barn owl	Peregrine
Barnacle goose	Pinkfoot goose
Bar-tailed godwit	Pintail
Curlew	Purple sandpiper
Dunlin	Red-breasted Merganser
Goldeneye	
Golden plover	Rock pipit
Great-crested grebe	Redshank
	Sanderling
Grey plover	Scaup
Greylag goose	Short-eared owl
Guillemot	Slavonic grebe
Hen harrier	Snow bunting
Kittiwake	Teal
Knot	Turnstone
Jacksnipe	Twite
Mallard	Whooper swan
Merlin	Wigeon

Summer Visitors

Common sandpiper
Common tern
Greenshank
Linnet
Little tern
Sedge warbler
Spotted redshank
Wood sandpiper
Wheatear
Whinchat

Huge numbers of species are recorded. For example, at South Walney observatory almost 200 varieties, including many wildfowl and waders, are recorded.

Passage Birds

Black-tailed godwit
Curlew sandpiper
Green sandpiper
Grey plover
Ruff
Turnstone
Whimbrel

Barnacle geese in flight at Caerlaverock

Mires & Meadows

Meadows: Grassland with high water-table. Much winter flooding. Important habitat for daily "commuting" waders and wildfowl, which fly between farmland and intertidal mudflats.
Mires: Four major bogs south of the Solway estuary. Largest remaining "raised bogs" in England. Acidic, saturated peat. Nutritionally poor, but important for some bird species

Landward of the Solway estuaries and salt marshes are the lush, grassy meadows and raised bogs or mires of the Solway Plain. The land here is only just above sea-level and water tables are high. During the winter many areas of the plain are flooded, and at spring tides, the sea penetrates far inland up the becks and ditches which normally provide drainage. In some places, wholesale inundation by the sea is only prevented by sea-dykes such as the one on the south side of Skinburness marsh.

The meadows provide a habitat which is totally complementary and in many ways essential to that of the estuarine mud-flats and salt marshes. Food in the meadows varies for different species, but includes worms, beetles, snails, cranefly larvae, flies, spiders, ants and slugs. Every day, and in some cases every tide, there is an exchange of birds between the two adjacent habitats.

Oystercatchers

Curlew

Snipe

Along the coast, the waders move up and down the beach with each rising and ebbing tide. At high tide, and especially during the height of the spring tides which flood the salt marshes, wading birds retire to feed inland, on the fields of the Solway Plain. Similarly, some of the gulls feed on the estuary and fly inland at high tide, and others feed in fields inland, flying back to the safety of the estuary at night. Interspersed amongst the pastures, are remains of originally larger areas of what are called "raised mires" or "bogs", locally known as "mosses", vast areas of highly acidic peat moss, domed up above the level of the surrounding land. The meadows are continuous, but the raised mires are reduced to a few substantial remnants at Drumburgh, Glasson, Bowness and Wedholme Flow (see photograph opposite), plus a number of smaller sites, located mainly between Abbeytown and Allonby. During much of the 20th century the mosses were exploited for agricultural peat, but in recent years water-tables have been raised again and attempts made to return the land to its former bog-like state.

Lapwing

Intertidal feeders which fly inland at high tide

Bar-tailed godwit
Curlew
Curlew sandpiper
Dunlin
Golden plover
Great black-backed gull
Green sandpiper
Grey plover
Herring gull
Knot
Lesser black-backed gull
Oystercatcher
Redshank
Ruff
Spotted redshank
Turnstone
Whimbrel

Landward Feeders which move to the estuary at night

Wildfowl, including:
Greylag goose
Mallard
Pinkfoot goose
Black-headed gull
Common gull
Herring gull

Other meadow birds

Summer visitors include:
Sedge warbler
Grasshopper warbler
Yellow wagtail

Other common birds
Pheasants
Snipe
Lapwings

Opposite: Wedholme Flow

Sea Cliffs

Essentials: Highest sea-cliffs on west coast of England are at St Bees Head, the most important breeding cliff for sea birds in the North-West. Wide range of species, full of noise and movement from March to midsummer, then quiet. Predators such as Peregrines prey on the mass of breeding birds.

Blencathra

The vast majority of birds are spring and summer visitors, using the cliffs as a nesting site. They arrive in early spring, and are gone again by the end of summer, creating a dramatic contrast between the unmistakable sounds and sights of a sea-bird cliff in spring, compared with its emptiness in winter.

Although there are some other small cliffs on the Cumbrian coast, this habitat is really about the red sandstone cliffs of St Bees Head, thrusting out into the Irish Sea. At almost 100 metres, the cliffs are the highest on the west coast of England and the most important sea-bird nesting cliff in northwest England.

Cliffs adjacent to the food source of the Irish Sea provide the ideal nesting site for many seabirds, along with their inevitable predators such as Peregrines and Kestrels.

Birds which breed at St Bees

Black guillemot
Fulmar
Great black-backed gull
Guillemot
Herring gull
Jackdaw
Kestrel
Kittiwake
Little owl
Merlin
Peregrine
Puffin
Raven
Razorbill
Rock pipit
Starling
Stock dove
Wren

The Puffin, everyone's favourite

Passage birds, early spring

House martin
Meadow pipit
Skylark
Stonechat
Swallow
Warblers, various
Whinchat

Visible out at sea from the cliff-top

The Isle of Man
Various divers
Gannets
Grebes
Skuas
Shearwater
Storm petrels
Terns, various
......plus many more.

Guillemots

Coastal Dunes

Essentials: Mixture of active dunes next to the sea, with fossil dunes and wetter dune "slacks" inland. Fairly impoverished bird habitat, but the choice of some species for breeding, often in large numbers.

Coastal dunes are created by sand blown up from the beach by the almost constant westerly wind. Those dunes nearest the sea are still active and subject to constant movement, but as you move landward there is generally a line of "fossilized" dunes, usually fixed with marram grass and heather, mostly calluna.

There are three main areas of dunes along the Cumbrian coast:
- Between Silloth and Maryport
- Around the combined mouths of the Rivers Esk, Mite and Irt, at Ravenglass
- Walney Island and Sandscale Haws

In general, dunes have no great attraction as an area where birds feed. However, many birds find them attractive for breeding. Dune breeders include Black-headed gulls, Lesser black-backed gulls and Herring gulls. Others include Skylarks, Shelducks and Red-breasted merganser.

The world's most southerly nesting colony of Eider ducks is on dunes at South Walney Island.

Dune Nesters
Arctic tern
Great black-backed gull
Herring gull
Lesser black-backed gull
Liitle tern
Meadow pipit
Sandwich tern
Skylark

Nesting ground on South Walney

Eider duck nesting

Eider duck family outing

Birds are not the only wildlife. We saw this adder on the dunes at Drigg.

Opposite: The beach at Sandscale Haws

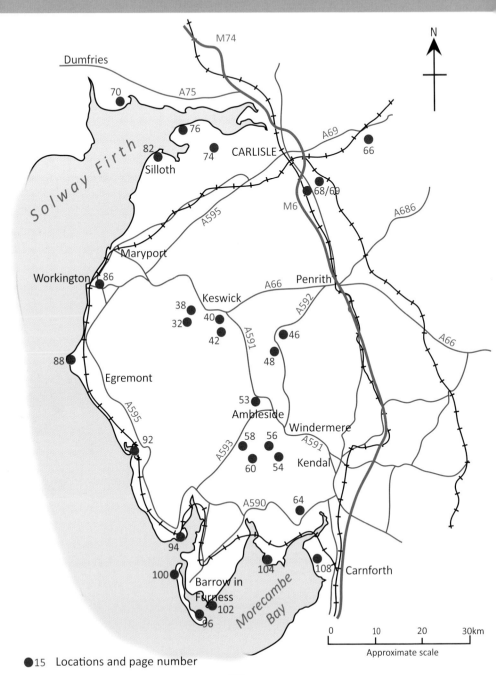

● 15   Locations and page number

30

Each location gets at least a double page, eg Siddick Ponds.

Name

Status and Management

Access

Main features

Habitat colour code

Special birds to look for

Photo giving a flavour of the site

Sketch map showing location

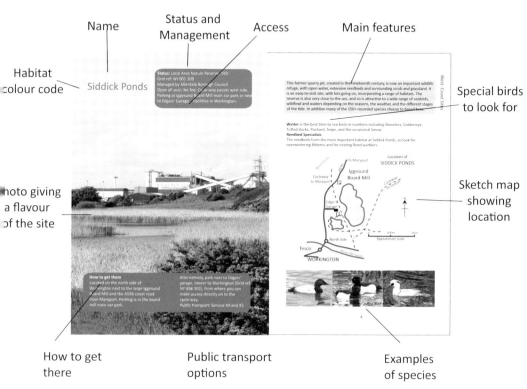

How to get there

Public transport options

Examples of species

ABBREVIATIONS EXPLAINED

AONB - Area of Outstanding Natural Beauty
NNR - National Nature Reserve
RSPB - Royal Society for the Protection of Birds
SAC - Special Area of Conservation
SPA - Special Protection Area
SSSI - Site of Special Scientific Interest

Sketch maps in Simple Guides are simplified maps showing only information necessary to navigate to each site. For more detail, refer to O.S. Landranger 85, 86, 89, 90, 91, 96 and 97.

LEGEND

The maps follow simple, normal map conventions for water, roads, tracks, woodland, marsh etc. Scales vary.
Note the following, specific symbols:

☼ Good birdwatching viewpoint

P Formal & informal parking for watching birds, accessing hides

Ⓗ Hide - usually a wooden structure for viewing wildlife.

The Osprey Project Bassenthwaite

The Lake District Osprey Project, is managed jointly by the Forestry Commission, the RSPB and the National Parks Authority. There are two locations, Dodd Wood for the osprey nest site and Whinlatter Visitor Centre for CCTV of the nest.

How to get there
Dodd Wood (Mirehouse)

Grid ref of car park: NY 234 281
From A66 roundabout northwest of Keswick, take the A591 north for about 3km (2 miles) to the well-signposted car park at Mirehouse. From here a steep path leads to the Lower Viewpoint, with views of the lake and ospreys fishing. The Upper Viewpoint, with views of the osprey nest, is another 800m uphill on a forest road.
To arrange for disabled access, phone 07899 818421.

Whinlatter Visitor Centre

Grid ref: NY 208 245
From the A66 west of Keswick west of Keswick, take the B5292 road through Braithwaite village to Whinlatter Pass. The visitor centre is well-signposted after about 3km (2 miles). Disabled access. Note that both these sites will be very busy especially at weekends and during holiday periods.
Public transport: Osprey Bus round Bassenthwaite from Keswick.
Service X4 Keswick to Cockermouth.

SOUTH BASSENTHWAITE LAKE

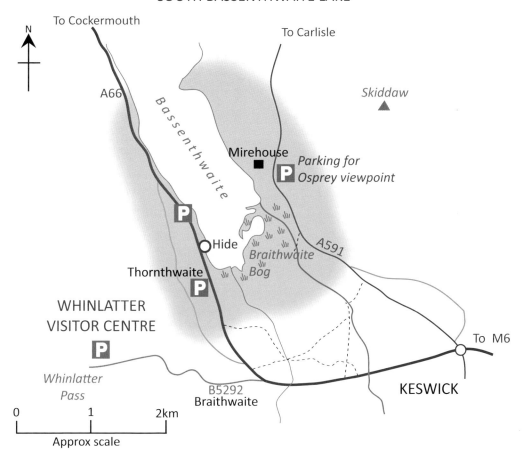

With the return of nesting ospreys to Bassenthwaite in 2001, followed by the recent re-introduction of Red kites at Grizedale, the Lake District is now the place to be for watching wild birds of prey. You can spend a whole day watching Bassenthwaite's ospreys, first at Dodd Wood and then at Whinlatter.

From the Dodd Wood (Mirehouse) car park the footpath climbs steeply to the Lower Viewpoint. Here you can look out over the lake, and often see the ospreys fishing or perching on posts at the edge of the water.

The Upper Viewpoint, with scopes and volunteers, gives a view of the nest which is about 400 metres away.

Both locations have scopes and binoculars available, and volunteer wardens at hand, ready to give advice.

Osprey's view of Bassenthwaite

The view you get of the osprey at the nest

Cafe at Dodd Wood

Part of the Whinlatter exhibition

Whinlatter has live CCTV from April to August, with advisers on hand to explain every piece of action on the nest, from mating, egg laying, hatching, feeding to fledging, an enthralling experience.

During the rest of the year, videos of the previous season are played.

The Osprey Story

In 2001, after an absence of 150 years, ospreys returned to nest in the Lake District. They did it with the help of a man-made nesting platform in Wythop Forest, on the western side of Bassenthwaite.

Ospreys had been seen flying over the area for several years, and indeed had returned to nest in Scotland in the 1950s. To encourage nesting, a series of artificial platforms was erected in various locations in the forest, with the aim of enticing a pair of birds to set up home. In 2001 it happened, and ospreys nested there until 2006. In 2007 they moved, but fortunately only to another prepared site, the present one, across the lake in Dodd Wood.

Look! I can fly!

Two or three eggs are laid at the end of April and hatch after 37 days, with the female doing most of the incubation. The young grow quickly, and after about 50 days are the size of their parents, and ready to fly. After another month or two, they are independent and ready for their 3000 mile journey southwards, leaving Bassenthwaite about the end of August.

The nest is huge, the size of a pallet, and is normally at the top of a tree, often a conifer. Perhaps it is not surprising that the occurrence of flat-topped mature trees is relatively rare in Britain, and so the most successful ospreys have been those receiving a helping hand from man with their nest-building, as with both nests so far used at Bassenthwaite.

There are three basic man-made nest models. Most common is the nest which purely mimics nature. The top of a large tree is trimmed, and an impression of a natural nest is created. However, ospreys also take to a "cradle" on the top of a pole, or even a nest built on an existing structure, like an electricity pylon. Not surprisingly, most of us prefer the natural model.

The Osprey Story (continued)

The osprey is a fish-eating raptor. In the bird of prey hierarchy, ospreys are medium-sized, with a wing span of about 1.8m (6 feet). After migrating south, they spend their first 3 years in the wetlands of West Africa, usually Senegal or Gambia. Then they return to UK or elsewhere in Europe, eventually to breed, though not necessarily in the first year of returning. They normally arrive at the end of March and stay until the end of August. Once mated they usually stay monogamous. However, if one of the pair fails to return, it is normal for the remaining bird to take another mate, as happened at Bassenthwaite in 2007. There are often other ospreys around, looking for a mate. They feed entirely on fish, plucked out of the water from a depth of up to a metre. In UK they prefer to fish for pike, perch and trout.

Mum brings a fish

The kids squabble over the food

More squabbling

Mum gives up and takes the fish away

Other UK ospreys

Ospreys are still very rare in England, with only a few nesting pairs. There are nests at Rutland Water and also in Kielder Forest in Northumberland.

Scotland is a different matter, with several hundred nests annually, the nearest to the Lake District being at Caerlaverock near Dumfries.

Ospreys first returned to nest at Loch Garten on Speyside in 1959, and to Loch of the Lowes in Perthshire, ten years later. Today there are ospreys in many places, and it is a common sight to see them fishing almost anywhere in Scotland.

Opposite: A natural nest in Perthshire

Bassenthwaite & Braithwaite Bog

Status: NNR, owned by the National Park
Fourth largest lake, and one of the best for birdwatching.
Totally accessible all year, mainly on the western shore.

How to get there

For Osprey Watching, see Osprey Project. Best access is along the western shore adjacent to the A66, and along the southern edge of Braithwaite Bog starting at Grid ref: NY 230 255 (on the A66) or on the A591 north of Keswick at Grid ref: NY 245 265.

A public hide, overlooking the southwest corner of the lake, and the edge of the Bog, is located south of Blackstock Point, accessed by walking from the parking at Grid ref: NY 219 276 or from Thornthwaite (Grid ref: NY 220 265). See map, page 33. Note that the footpath along the southern edge of the Bog may be intermittently flooded, especially in winter.

Public transport: Osprey Bus (Round Bassenthwaite from Keswick) Services X5 and X4 Keswick to Cockermouth.

The southern end of nutrient-rich Bassenthwaite, together with adjacent Braithwaite bog, provides the best general birdwatching experience in the Lake District, and has interest at all seasons. Bassenthwaite was, only a few thousand years ago, part of a much bigger lake, including Derwentwater to the south. Today the southern end is shallow, with the little deltas of the River Derwent and the Newlands beck, ideal habitat for all manner of waterfowl. Beyond the lake is perhaps the biggest area of wetland in the Lake District, vegetated with reedbeds, birch and alder. It is largely isolated, with few paths and therefore little disturbance - a bird haven.

Birds to look for
Spring and summer.

Look out for Ospreys fishing. (see Osprey Project)

There are over 70 breeding species of birds here. Along the edges of lake and the bog, especially look for Reed warbler, Yellow wagtail, Water rail, Grasshopper warbler, Chiffchaff, Willow warbler and most of the tits.

Common sandpiper, Great-crested and little grebe. Red-breasted merganser and Goosander may be present year-round. Look out for Snipe and Dipper, and for Buzzard and other raptors hunting over both lake and bog.

Dippers

Autumn and winter

During the winter the lake may have over 2,000 ducks, including Goldeneye, Tufted ducks, Pochard, Wigeon, Teal and the ubiquitous Mallard. Seabirds, including a variety of gulls, use the lake especially when conditions at sea are stormy.

David Feltham

Sedge warbler

Goldeneye

Pochard

Tufted duck

Derwentwater

Status: SSSI and SAC
Most of the eastern side is owned
and managed by the National Trust.

How to get there

Park in the car park at Keswick south of the town centre next to the theatre and the Derwentwater landing stage. Grid ref: NY 266 229. Take the path along the lakeside signed for Friar's Crag, which at least to the crag is wheelchair friendly. A path continues, sometimes by the lake, sometimes in the woods across the road, all the way to Borrowdale. If you go as far as Lodore, we suggest a return by Keswick launch on a boat taking the clockwise route.

Note that the car park and pathways will be very busy during holiday periods and on many weekends throughout the year.

Public transport: Services X4 X5 from Penrith or Cockermouth, plus others.

Derwentwater is one of the shallowest lakes, and is well on the way to being filled in with sediment. It is also one of the most nutritional lakes, with lots of aquatic life and food for birds. The eastern shore, from Keswick southwards is also one of the busiest areas, especially the short walk to the iconic Friar's Crag, so do not expect to do your birdwatching here in solitude. All the same, there is a surprising amount of bird life both on the water and in the adjacent woods. (see Borrowdale Woods page 43)

To the south of the lake is a wetland, located in front of the Lodore Hotel, with access using the path crossing the valley bottom via Chinese Bridge. This path also skirts round the edge of Great Bay, which is generally avoided by lake users because of its special conservation status.

The ubiquitous Mallard

Birds to look out for
(especially in winter)

Black-headed gull	Greylag goose
Coot	Mallard
Cormorants	Pochard
Goldeneye	Tufted duck
Grey heron	

Cormorant

Grey heron

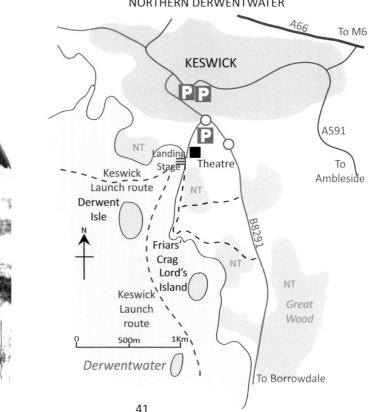

NORTHERN DERWENTWATER

A66
To M6

KESWICK

A591

To Ambleside

NT

Landing Stage

Theatre

Keswick Launch route

Derwent Isle

NT

B8291

N

Friars' Crag

Lord's Island

NT

NT

Great Wood

Keswick Launch route

0   500m   1Km

Derwentwater

To Borrowdale

41

Borrowdale Woods

Status: SSSI and SAC
National Trust Reserve
Parking generally National Trust pay and display.
Accessible all year.

How to get there

Grid ref: NY 267196 (most northern car park); most southern car park, NY 246 137. Located between the southern end of Derwentwater and the southern end of Borrowdale, on either side of the B5289, which runs from Keswick, over Honister Pass to Buttermere. Leave Keswick from the roundabout near to the lake and the theatre. Car parks are generally Pay and Display, National Trust, free to members. Also accessible by Keswick Launch from Keswick Landing, calling at Lodore and High/Low Brandelhowe. Public transport service 78, Keswick to Seatoller.

This is the largest remaining area of semi-natural woodland in the Lake District: mixed deciduous woods, with Sessile oak predominant. There are 6 or 7 sections, more or less joined together. Though there is an excellent and popular path network, including the Cumbria Way, many woods are located on steep, rocky slopes, with difficult access. However, there is a good path network in both Lodore Woods in the northeast, and Johnny's Wood near Seatoller.

Birds to look for

Refer to Habitat and Species, p16 & 17. The main mixed woodland species, especially include:
Buzzard, Great-spotted woodpecker, Pied flycatcher, Tawny owl, Treecreeper, Tree pipit, Wood warbler.

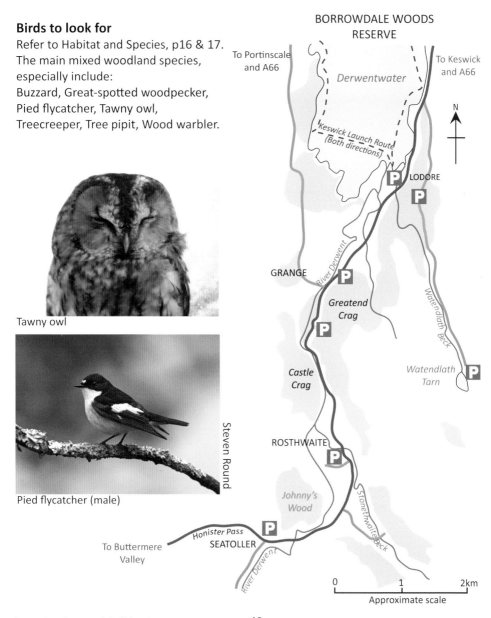

Tawny owl

Pied flycatcher (male)

BORROWDALE WOODS RESERVE

To Portinscale and A66

Derwentwater

To Keswick and A66

N

Keswick Launch Route (Both directions)

P   LODORE
    P

River Derwent

GRANGE   P

Greatend Crag

Watendlath Beck

P

Castle Crag

Watendlath Tarn   P

Steven Round

ROSTHWAITE   P

Johnny's Wood

Stonethwaite Beck

Honister Pass   P
SEATOLLER

To Buttermere Valley

River Derwent

0   1   2km
Approximate scale

Linskeldfield Tarn

Status: Private Nature Reserve
Managed by farm owners.
Parking: Free to Reserve, but donations welcome.
Self-catering accommodation.
Nearest facilities: at Castle Inn on Keswick road.

How to get there

Located about 6 miles east of Cockermouth on the north side of the river Derwent, less than a mile south of the village of Sunderland.
Easiest approach is off the A591, Keswick to Carlisle road, at Grid Ref: NY 185 376. Take the road to Sunderland. After about 1km (0.75 miles), you will find Linskeldfield on your left.
There are no public transport options.

LInskeldfield Tarn is a farm wetland which has been dammed and turned into an important wildlife habitat. In addition, the owners have recently created a modern, 12-person hide.

This is one of these hidden-away gems, where you can find wildlife, and peace and quiet, away from the hustle and bustle of Keswick, Cockermouth and Catbells, but "just down the road". With three self-catering farm cottages, recently converted from farm buildings, this is an ideal location for a birdwatching break. See www.linskeldfield.co.uk

Birds to look out for:

Over 90 species of waders and wildfowl have been identified, especially the following:

Cormorant
Gadwall
Goldeneye
Lapwing
Little grebe
Oystercatcher
Pintail
Pochard
Shelduck
Shoveler
Whooper swan
Wigeon

There are also otters and red squirrels.

Canada geese breed at Linskeldfield

Location of Linskeldfield

View from the hide

Opposite: Canada goose on the move

Ullswater

Status: Owned and managed by the Lake District National Park Authority.
Second largest lake after Windermere.
Parking and facilities at various points along the lake, with best road access on the north and west sides.

How to get there

Arrive from the M6, A66 or from Windermere and Ambleside via the A592, the latter over Kirkstone Pass.

There are many parking places along the north and west side of the lake. They are busy during weekends and the holiday season, especially at Aira Force, but quieter during the rest of the year.

The road on the south and east side of the lake, from Pooley Bridge to Sandwick has less access to the lake and few parking places.

Public transport: Service 108 Penrith to Patterdale. Service 517 Windermere to Patterdale.

As Ullswater is too large for comprehensive coverage here, we shall suggest just two locations which have proved fruitful.

a) Park at the National Trust Aira Force car park (Grid ref: NY 401 200) and follow the paths either side of the Aira Beck.

b) Park across the road from the Patterdale Hotel, (Grid ref: NY397157). Walk back in the direction of Glenridding for 100m and take the path across the valley bottom. At the farm on the far side, turn left. This path eventually leads to Sandwick, but passes through a mixture of rich habitat along the way

The lake is generally very deep, but the many sheltered bays, and the mainly oak and birch woodland can be rewarding for the birdwatcher.

Birds to look out for

There is a good range of woodland birds, including Pied flycatcher, Siskin, Nuthatch, Great-spotted woodpecker, Treecreeper, Redpoll, Redstart, and Tawny owl.

Water birds are best in winter, especially a huge roost on the water of Black-headed and Common gulls. Wildfowl include a wide range of ducks, including Mallard, Wigeon, Tufted duck and Goldeneye, as well as Whooper swans, Greylag geese and the ubiquitous Cormorant. Peregrines breed on the surrounding crags.

Around the lake there are breeding Grey wagtails, Dipper, Pied wagtail, Coot, Red-breasted merganser, Redshank and lots of others.

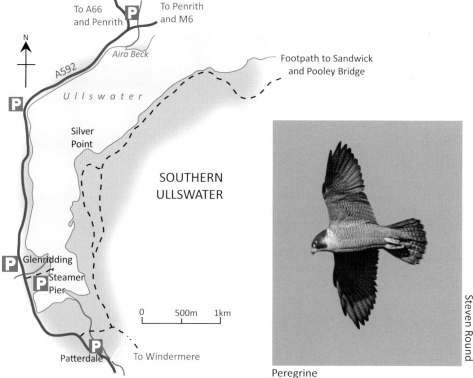

Peregrine

Steven Round

47

Brotherswater

Status: SSSI
Owned and managed by the National Trust.
Parking to north of lake, currently free.

How to get there
Grid ref: NY 403 134 (car park). Busy in holiday season. Located next to the A592 road from Ullswater to Windermere via Kirkstone Pass. The car park is just 500 metres north of the lake. A good path runs along the lake's western edge, also giving access to Low Wood and to Dovedale. Public transport: Service 108, Penrith - Patterdale and Service 517, Windermere - Patterdale.

Brotherwater is a fine place to birdwatch. It is one of the smallest lakes, and this, combined with a path on the western side, between the water and the woods, makes it an easy place to watch the wealth of birds. This is a nutrient-rich lake, and it also has wetlands at both ends, with reedbeds to the south, and wet grassland to the north, allowing for a wide range of residents and migrants. Low Wood, immediately to the west, and Dovedale to the south increase the possibilities.

There is a nice picnic spot at the southwest corner of the lake, and food and refreshments are available at Brotherswater Inn opposite the lake on A592.

Birds to look out for around the lake and in Low Wood

Residents	Winter Visitors	Summer Visitors
Buzzard	Fieldfare	Common sandpiper
Dipper	Goldeneye	Grey wagtail
Goosander	Greylag goose	Pied flycatcher
Gt-sp'd woodpecker	Pinkfoot	Redstart
Grey heron	Pochard	Ring ouzel
Little grebe	Red-breasted merganser	Sedge warbler
Nuthatch	Redpoll	Yellow wagtail
Peregrine	Redwing	Wheatear
Reed bunting	Shoveller	Whinchat
Snipe	Siskin	
Treecreeper	Wigeon	

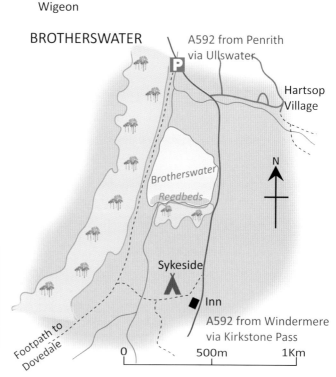

BROTHERSWATER

A592 from Penrith via Ullswater

Hartsop Village

Brotherswater Reedbeds

N

Sykeside

Inn

A592 from Windermere via Kirkstone Pass

Footpath to Dovedale

0   500m   1Km

Goldeneye

Pied wagtail

Opposite: North end of Brotherswater

Haweswater

Status: RSPB Reserve
The only place in England where you might reliably see a Golden Eagle.
Parking. No facilities, though Haweswater Hotel is situated half way along the lake.

How to get there

Grid reference of parking: NY 469 107
Best find your way off the M6 at junction 39. Proceed to the north end of Shap village, and turn left for Burnbank and Haweswater. At Burnbank, take the road along the south shore of the lake until you reach the car park at the southern end.

Then walk around the lake, crossing the ridge just before the wood. The hide, and the furthest point you are allowed to go, is a few hundred metres beyond the small stone barn, which many may initially mistake for the hide.
Public transport only infrequently to Burnbanks from Penrith, service 111.

At the time of writing, there is only one eagle, a male, at Haweswater, who still displays in the spring, in the hope of attracting a passing female. The RSPB hide is located at the foot of Riggindale, below Rough Crag, and offers the best chance of seeing the bird.

There is a part-time warden, usually there at weekends and bank holidays, who will help you spot the eagle, but it is best to check. Seeing a Golden eagle may require considerable patience and is not guaranteed. Most likely any view will be in silhouette, when the bird breaks the skyline either displaying or hunting.

Even if you fail to see the eagle, this is a lovely area to visit, just for the drive, or for a walk or a picnic.

Other birds you may see

Fellside & Crags	Surrounding Woodlands	Lake
Peregrine	Buzzard	Range of ducks
Kestrel	Sparrowhawk	Greylag geese
Raven	Gt-spotted woodpecker	Canada geese
Ring ouzel	Spotted flycatcher	Breeding gulls (various)
Wheatear	Woodcock	Winter roosts of Common & Black-headed gulls

Golden eagle

The classical Golden eagle silhouette

RSPB HIDE
RIGGINDALE

To Burnbank and Shap

N

Riggindale Beck

Hide   Stone Barn

Haweswater Reservoir

Riggindale Crag

Mardale Common

Footpath to High Street

P

0   500m
Approx scale

Opposite: The hide at the foot of the crags   51

Rydal Water

Status: Managed by RSPB and National Park Authority.
Lake; deciduous woods; open fellside.
Parking; good path system; Information.
Facilities in Rydal village, Grasmere and also in Ambleside.

How to get there

Located between Ambleside and Grasmere on the A591. Highly accessible and busy at weekends and during holidays.
Best parking is at Whitemoss Common, on either side of the road (Grid ref: NY 349 065) Take the path south of the road which leads around the lake. If you follow the path in an anti-clockwise direction, it will bring you back to the A591 at the foot of the road to Rydal Mount, Wordsworth's final home. Walk up the road and take the path to the left, beyond Rydal Mount, back below Nab Scar to the White Moss carparks.
Public transport: Service 555 Kendal-Windermere-Keswick. Train to Windermere.

Rydal and the countryside around it are beautiful, and it was Wordsworth's favourite lake. So it is a tourist hotspot. However, this does not detract from it being a fine birdwatching location at all seasons. If you don't like crowds, avoid the obviously busy times.

Within a small area you will find remarkably varied habitat. From the lake and fen at its west end, to mainly oak woodland, which is sometimes quite open, to typical fellside. So there is a wide range of birds.

Birds to look out for

Birds which are there all year include: Heron, Dipper and Grey wagtail along the lake edge: Coot, Moorhen, Greylag and Canada geese on the water. In the woods and open fell look out for Jay, Ravens, Stonechat, Treecreeper, Nuthatch and Goldcrest, Green and Great-spotted woodpeckers, together with the resident raptors, Peregrine, Kestrel and Buzzard.

In Spring and Summer, enjoy Swallows, Swifts and Sandmartins over the lake, Wheatear on the open fell, and Pied and Spotted flycatcher, Tree pipit , Whinchat and Redstart in the woods.

In Winter you are always likely to see a range of ducks such as Goldeneye, Tufted duck, Pochard and Goosander, as well as Cormorants. In the woods, look out for winter visitors such as Brambling, and the members of the Thrush family such as Redwing and Fieldfare, as they forage for berries.

RYDAL WATER

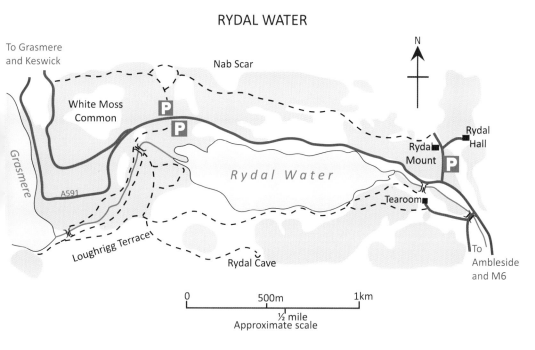

Windermere

This is the largest lake, and most important for waterbird numbers.
Parking and good birding spots are at National Park Centre at Brockhole, Waterhead at Ambleside and at the southern end, at Lakeside.

How to get there
At over 10 miles long (17km), Windermere is the largest lake, and there are lots of points of access.
Generally arrive on the A591 from Kendal, the A592 from Newby Bridge, and from Penrith. There are good access points at **the** National Park Centre at Brockhole **(**Grid ref: NY 390 010), at Ambleside, north and south from the western terminal of the Windermere ferry, and around the lake.
Public transport: Service 555 Kendal to Keswick.
Train: Kendal to Windermere.

Windermere is the largest lake in England, and is well-wooded on its banks, especially on the western side. Its combination of reedy bays and lots of islands make for a series of encouraging bird habitats. Yet sometimes we tend to ignore it for birdwatching, as it is the most commercialised of the lakes, and there is so much else going on. Although there is a good range of birds all year, (the National Park claim over 1000 resident ducks and swans) as with most of the lakes, the autumn and winter see the biggest influx, and numbers rise to over 2,500 waterbirds.

Top Birds
This is one of the top locations in the country for spotting Goldeneye, Red-breasted merganser, Coot, Tufted duck and Pochard.

Other birds to look out for
There are always hundreds of friendly Mallard ducks, Mute swan, (our biggest bird), attractive Great-crested grebes, which are spectacular in spring courtship, Cormorants, Canada geese, often huge gull roosts, plus a wide range of other ducks and geese. If you are able to do so, check out the sheltered, shallow reedy places on the edge of the lake.
Most of the surrounding woodland is deciduous. Check out bird species in the Habitats-Species section pages 16-17.

Great-crested grebe

Mute swan

Windermere at Bowness

Goldeneye

55

Esthwaite Water

Status: NNR at North Fen, on north edge of lake; SSSI.
Managed by English Nature
WWF Ecological score of 4 (high quality)
Limited parking at south end of lake, other parking **and
facilities in nearby Hawkshead.**

How to get there

Esthwaite Water is located just south of the village of Hawkshead accessed on the B5285 from Ambleside, or via the Winder-mere ferry through Near and Far Sawrey. Parking is limited at the southern end (Grid ref: SD 361 954), though there are public roads surrounding the lake.

A public footpath goes from the southern end of Hawkshead to the head of the lake. Public transport: Service 505 Ambleside to Hawkshead. Services X30 and X31 from Hawkshead.

Esthwaite Water was probably the favourite lake of Beatrix Potter, who lived in nearby Hilltop in Far Sawrey. She used the lake as the home of one of her famous characters, the waistcoat-wearing frog, Mr Jeremy Fisher.

Esthwaite is one of Lakeland's most nutritious lakes. It is only about 6m (approx 20ft) deep, and supports a wealth of plant life, invertebrates and fish. It is therefore a superb place for birdwatching. At the northern end is North Fen, an area of peat, reedbeds and oak woodland, which provides an important habitat. North Fen is viewable from the B5285 to the west of the lake, or from the public footpath.

Birds to look out for

Look out for nesting Great-crested and Little grebes. In the reeds check for Sedge warblers and Reed buntings.

In winter there will usually be a good range of ducks such as Mallard, Goldeneye, Scaup and Scoter, as well as Red-breasted merganser and Water rail.

Great-crested grebe

Goldeneye

Location of ESTHWAITE

Coniston Water

Status: Owned and managed by National Park.
Third largest lake in Lake District.
Many parking spots especially on eastern side.
Best birdwatching is in quieter south.
Facilities in Coniston village and at Brantwood.

How to get there

Generally accessed from Ambleside, using the A593/A508, or from the Southern Lakes road, the A590, via Penny Bridge. Best to go to quieter southern end, especially the eastern shore north of High Nibthwaite, where there are many parking spots on the lake side.

There are also launches around most of the lake - see Coniston Launch website.

Public transport: Either service X12 or 505 between Ambleside and Ulverston.

Coniston Water is a good spot to view water-birds especially in winter. The eastern shore is also the western edge of Grizedale Forest, and has a good range of birds of both deciduous and coniferous woodland.

We suggest you generally avoid the busier northern area, which is very busy with boating during much of the year.

Birds to look for

All year: Look along the water edge for Dippers, Grey wagtails, Pied wagtails and Herons. There are plenty of raptors hunting or scavenging around the lake, including Peregrines, Buzzards and Sparrowhawks.

On the water there are always Canada geese and Greylags, also a variety of resident ducks and Red-breasted mergansers.

Look out for Red kites, recently released at Grizesdale.

Winter: The best time, with a wide range of ducks, including Wigeon, Pochard, Goldeneye, Gadwall, Teal and Shoveler: also Little and Great-crested grebe and Jack snipe.

In the eastern woodlands look out for Waxwings, Short-eared owls, Crossbill, Nuthatches and Siskins.

Summer: Look out for the migrants coming here to nest, including a range of warblers, Pied flycatcher and the various Pipits. Ospreys are already seen fishing in the lake and hopefully will soon nest here.

Canada goose

SOUTH
CONISTON WATER

Coniston Water

Rigg Wood
P

To Coniston
and Ambleside

(may be closed following privatisation)

GRIZEDALE
P FOREST

Thrang Crag
Wood
P

P

A5084

N

P

High
Nibthwaite

Water
Yeat

To A590
and M6

0   1   2km

Approximate scale

Siskin

Wigeon

Opposite page: Brown Howe, Coniston Water   59

Grizedale Forest

Status: Forest Park, over 3000 hectares. Managed by Forestry Commission Excellent facilities include: parking, toilets, trails, wheelchair access, picnic sites, interpretive signs etc.
Contact: 01229 860010

How to get to the Grizedale Centre
Grid ref: SD 335 945
From Ambleside, use the A591, then the B5286 to Hawkshead, and take the minor road to Grizedale and Satterthwaite for about 2 miles.
From the south (M6) take the A590 past Newby Bridge, then at Haverthwaite turn right to "Grizedale Forest Park" and Satterthwaite.
Public transport: Service 505 Ambleside to Hawshead; services X30 and X31 from Hawkshead.

Grizedale is the largest continuous area of forest in the Lake District. Trees are largely coniferous, but there are also over 700 acres of deciduous woodland, especially oak. Different tree species of different ages give rise to a wide variety of birds, and ponds and tarns created around the forest attract a range of water birds. We suggest you follow all or part of the Silurian Trail. (See map for route)

Birds to look out for

In Section 1 we explained the attraction of different stages of plantation and afforestation to different groups of birds. This helps to understand the range of species one might expect in different parts of Grizedale Forest. In the conifers look out for uncommon varieties such as Crossbills, Nuthatch and Long-eared owls. Hawfinch are found in mature oak woods, and Woodcock are common. Grizedale is also home to many of the common woodland species, to a range of ducks and waterbirds, and most of the raptors.

However, the main attraction in the coming years, as they establish and breed, will be the Grizedale Red kites.

GRIZEDALE FOREST
AND SILURIAN WAY

N

To Hawkshead
and Ambleside

GRIZEDALE
VISITOR CENTRE
Toilets
Information
Picnic Area
Cafe

To Hawkshead

Carron Crag

Silurian Way

GRIZEDALE
FOREST
PARK

Bogle
Crag

Silurian Way

David Feltham

Crossbill

Nuthatch

Steven Round

Lowdale
Park

To Penny Bridge
A590 and M6

Force Mills

To A590

0   1km   2km
Approx scale

Red Kites
Foraging Sequence

1

3

4

5

6

7

Red Kites back in the Lake District.

In 2010, an exciting experiment to re-introduce Red Kites to northwest England saw the release of the first 30 of a planned 90 birds in Grizedale.

Red Kites were once a common sight in Britain, but persecution by farmers and gamekeepers left them hanging on only in mid-Wales. Such persecution was sad and also misinformed, as Red Kites are mainly scavengers rather than hunters. But several re-introduction programmes have now occurred throughout the UK, and the Grizedale experiment is one of the last pieces in the jigsaw.

The birds released in 2010 all have a blue tag on their right wing and an orange tag on their left wing. Look out for them as you walk through the forest. Their long, forked tail makes them stand out from other birds of prey.

Right: Sequence of crows around a Red kite, and they can often be seen "mobbing" them in the air. Crows see Red kites as a threat (see below).

Some Red Kite Facts
(from Grizedale Red Kite Project)

Description
Wingspan: approximately 140-170 cm
Body Length: approximately 60-72 cm
A rich rufous brown and black plumage with large "windows" on under-wings
Long forked tail
Little difference between sexes
Largely silent

Diet and Feeding
Adults require 80-12g (3-5 oz) of food per day, equivalent to the weight of 2 or 3 voles.
Red Kites are mainly scavengers, largely relying on carrion. However, they do take some live prey, including rabbits, crows, rooks and jackdaws, pigeons, small mammals and invertebrates.
www.forestry.gov.uk/grizedalehome

Whitbarrow

Status: NNR, SSSI and SAC: Combination of National Nature Reserve and Hervey Memorial Reserve. Owned and managed by Forestry Commission, Lake District National Park and Cumbria Wildlife Trust. Most is open access. Parking in various locations both east and west side (refer to map)
Facilities in Witherslack village or at Lindale.

How to get there

Western side is accessed off A590 at Townend, through Witherslack village to parking just south of Witherslack Hall School (Grid ref: SD 437 860). A marked path leads steeply uphill to the top of Whitbarrow Scar. Or continue to North Lodge, where another path leads up to Scar and Wakebarrow Wood.

For the more gentle approaches on the eastern side, leave the A590 via the A5074 and park at one of the car parks shown on the map.

Public transport only to Witherslack, Service X35 from Kendal.

The Carboniferous limestone pavement and escarpment of Whitbarrow is different from almost all other Lake District habitats. Its geology gives it a quite different flora in comparison with the northern and central Lakeland woods. At Whitbarrow, ash replaces oak as the dominant tree, and there is often a dense and tangled understorey, especially of hazel, and so one can expect a different bird population.

In addition, the limestone pavement of the plateau is quite fascinating from a botanical viewpoint. The sheltered world of the cracks (called grikes) between the limestone blocks (called clints) harbours its own flora, with plants such as Wood anemones, Green spleenwort and Mountain avens.

Whitbarrow Scar also commands good views of Morecambe Bay to the south.

Birds to look out for

Birds will vary from the scar to the open limestone plateau, and from the woodlands on the scarp (steep) slope, to the woodland on the dip (gentle) slope. However, on your walk look out for the following.

All year round: Great-spotted and Green woodpeckers, Jays, Marsh tit, Long-tailed tit, Coaltit, Goldcrest, Nuthatch, Treecreeper, Redpoll, Skylark and Raven.

Also look out for predators like Peregrine, Buzzard and Sparrowhawk, especially on the cliffs.

In spring and summer, visitors arrive to nest. They include Wheatear, Chiffchaff, Spotted flycatcher and Willow warbler.

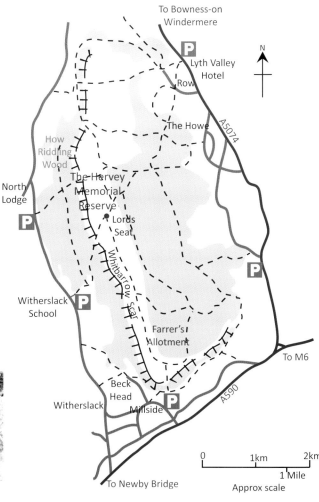

WHITBARROW

Vegetation in a grike

Opposite page: Whitbarrow Scar

Geltsdale

Status: AONB, SSSI, SAC, RSPB Reserve
Parking, trails and paths.
Interpretation Centre and toilets at Stagsike Cottages.
Reserve open at all times. Information centre, 9am - 5pm.
No admission charge, though donations are appreciated.

How to get there

Geltsdale is a huge reserve in the north Pennines, to the southeast of Brampton. There are various possible routes, but we suggest starting at the official RSPB car park, (Grid ref: NY 588 584).

Leave the A69 east of Brampton, and take the A689 to Hallbankgate and Alston. At Hallbankgate take the minor road past The Belted Will pub and continue to its end at Clesketts. From here there are, four way-marked trails, each one taking at least several hours, so bring adequate footwear and clothing, especially in winter. The Stagsike Trail is the shortest, and will take 1 – 2 hours.

It is possible to arrange access for disabled visitors : Tel: 016977 46717

Public transport: Services 685 to Brampton, 680 Brampton to Alston (Hallbankgate).

In comparison with other reserves, at 5,000 acres, Geltsdale is huge. It is the best moorland environment in Cumbria, with a mixture of heather, acid grassland and bog, and the only area where you have a reliable chance of seeing a good variety of moorland species. In addition there is considerable habitat diversity, with a mixture of upland hay meadow and recently planted woodland. Hardy upland cattle have largely displaced sheep, to provide a much richer grassland habitat.

The area is so big that birdwatching there is a true wilderness experience. The few other people there will be well-scattered, and it is a real opportunity to "get-away-from-it-all".

If you are lucky, you might see Hen harriers. This is one of only two places in England where Hen harriers have bred in the last ten years.

Birds to look out for

(See possible species in "moorland" in Habitats section)

Barn owls
Black grouse
Curlews
Hen harriers
Lapwings
Redshank
Predators such as Kestrel, Buzzard, Peregrine and Merlin.

At the time of writing, there was CCTV monitoring of a barn owl nest in the roof space of Stagsike Cottages.

Black grouse

Curlew

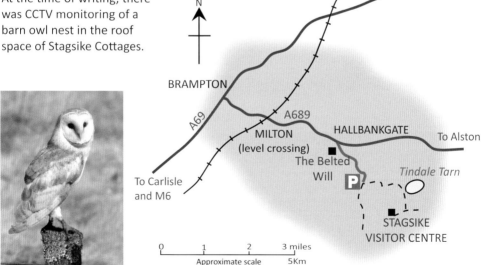
LOCATION OF GELTSDALE

To Hexham
N
BRAMPTON
A69
A689
MILTON
(level crossing)
HALLBANKGATE
To Alston
The Belted Will
Tindale Tarn
To Carlisle and M6
STAGSIKE VISITOR CENTRE

0   1   2   3 miles
Approximate scale   5Km

Barn owl

Opposite page: Stagsike meadow

Quarry Banks
and
Wreay Woods

Quarry Banks: managed by Cumbria Wildlife Trust. 1.8 hectares of mature, naturalised deciduous woodland, and unimproved grass.
Paths with steep slopes and stiles. Information boards.
Open all year: No charge, no facilities.
Not disabled-friendly.
Wreay Woods: managed by Cumbria Wildlife Trust.
Mature woodland; gorge of River Petteril; 17.7 ha.
Parking; paths; picnic site; information boards.
Other facilities in Carlisle.

Quarry Banks: How to get there
Access from Cumwhinton village, 2km (1.2 miles) east of M6 junction 42 on B6263. Turn right in village on Armathwaite Road and park. Take signed footpath east between houses, across Chestnut Grove, and 200m along pasture field to woods.

Wreay Woods: How to get there
Either take Dalston road for 200m off M6 junction 42. Turn left into parking and picnic area, then path under moptorway. Or, from junction 42 take A6 towards Penrith for 2km (1.2 miles). Park on left and cross road to access woods past Scalesceugh Hall.

Quarry Banks is a tiny reserve set around an abandoned sandstone quarry. The woodland has been allowed to naturalise, and there are nesting boxes everywhere. A little gem.

Wreay Woods is a remnant of a much larger forest, following the gorge of the River Petteril. Go in the spring and enjoy not only the sound and sight of the birds, but also carpets of Bluebells and other spring flowers.

Birds to look out for
Blackcap
Grey wagtail
Long-tailed tit
Spotted flycatcher
Treecreeper.
Dipper
Kestrel
Kingfisher
Tawny owl
Great-spotted woodpecker

Quarry Banks

Quarry Banks nesting boxes

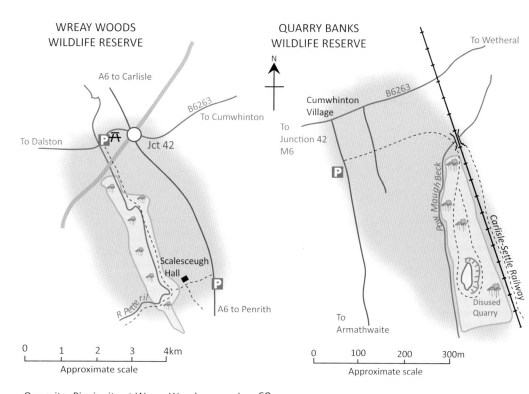

WREAY WOODS
WILDLIFE RESERVE

QUARRY BANKS
WILDLIFE RESERVE

Opposite: Picnic site at Wreay Woods car park   69

Caerlaverock

Status: Caerlaverock Wildfowl and Wetlands Trust (WWT) Reserve, NNR and SSSI. Grid ref. of centre: NY 051 656 Managed by the UK Wildfowl and Wetlands Trust. 587 hectares (1400 acres) of grassland and salt marsh. The only Scottish WWT centre out of nine in the UK.

How to get there
Located at East Park Farm, on the Solway coast, southeast of Dumfries. Approach from the A75, following signposts just west of Annan.

Alternatively, follow the B725 road southwards from central Dumfries. Then look out for the "Caerlaverock WWT" signposts.

Most people will realise that Caerlaverock is neither on the coast of Cumbria, nor even in England, but it is such an important and integral part of the Solway ecosystem that we decided to "borrow" it just for the book. In addition, at certain times, it is one of UK's best birdwatching experiences.

Caerlaverock has three core attractions. Firstly, the Svalbard population of well over 25,000 Barnacle geese return to Caerlaverock and the surrounding Solway coast every October. Secondly, the area is internationally important for over-wintering of a host of other wildfowl and wading birds.

Thirdly, in 2009, Ospreys successfully bred at Caerlaverock, the first in Dumfriesshire for over 100 years. The Visitor Centre has round-the-clock CCTV monitoring of the nest, and vistors can observe all stages in the annual breeding, with eggs being laid at the end of April, and the birds migrating to West Africa around the end of August.

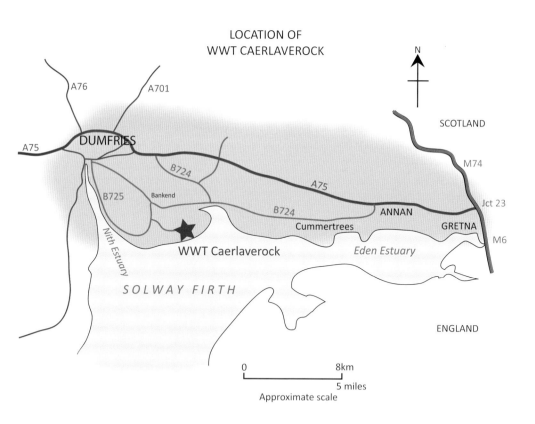

LOCATION OF
WWT CAERLAVEROCK

Opposite: Looking north from Caerlaverock   71

Brian Morrell

Large flock of Barnacle geese in front of the Farmhouse Tower

Barnacle geese

In the 1940s approximately 500 Barnacle geese found their way from Svalbard to winter in the Solway. However, today over 25,000 make the flight from Norway's Arctic outpost to winter at Caerlaverock and the rest of the Solway marshes. Visitors between October and April are more or less assured to see enormous flocks of these beautiful black and white geese.

Barnacle geese grazing

Birds to look out for

October to April, up to 25,000 Barnacle geese, plus hundreds of Whooper swans, and wildfowl and waders in great variety. From April to August, you will be able to view Caerlaverock's own osprey nest on CCTV.

Caerlaverock has seven full-time staff and 15 volunteers and is open every day except Christmas Day, 09.00–17.00. There is involvement in major education programmes, with a full-time "Learning Officer". A range of events and activities is on offer.

The excellent facilities include parking, coffee shop and gift shop, toilets, conference facilities, wheelchair-friendly trails, hides and observation towers. There is B & B accommodation next to the site.

Left: CCTV monitoring of the Osprey nest
Top: The coffee shop and gallery seating
Above: The conference room

PLAN OF RESERVE

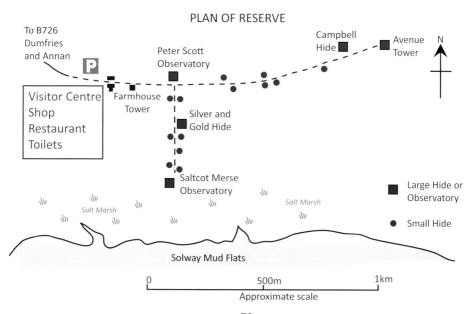

Finglandrigg Wood

Status: National Nature Reserve; SSSI
Managed by English Nature.
Best in Spring and Summer.
Parking. Good trails; boardwalks; picnic site.
Open all year; no access fee.

How to get there
Located 13km (about 8 miles) west of Carlisle on the B5307. Park at the lay-by 1.5km (about 1 mile) west of Kirkbampton village, and take the path into the reserve on the same side of the road.

From Wigton, take the road to Kirkbride, then turn right on the B5307 towards Carlisle for 5km (3 miles). Immediately after the woodland, park in the lay-by on the right, see map on page 77.
Partially wheelchair friendly.

Finglandrigg is one of the largest remaining areas of semi-natural woodland in the mainly grassland-pasture of the Solway Plain. In addition to the woodland, there is heathland, peatbog and rough pasture. It is important as an "island" habitat, with the next substantial woodland being several kilometres away.

It is a nice, family-friendly visit for summer outings, with good paths and a picnic site.

Birds to look out for.

Finglandrigg has over 40 nesting species.
Especially look for:

Curlew	Reed bunting
Garden warbler	Sparrowhawk
Grasshopper warbler	Tawny owl
Long-tailed tit	Common buzzard
Willow tit	

Steven Round

Picnic area

Goldfinch

Bullfinch

Sparrowhawk

Blue tit

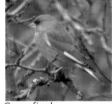

Greenfinch

Evidence of sparrowhawk's dinner?

You may also see Red squirrels and Roe deer.

Opposite: Birdwatching is for families

The Solway Peninsula

The Solway Peninsula, located between the Eden Estuary and Moricambe Bay, (the combined estuaries of the Waver and the Wampool rivers) is one of the most important birdwatching locations in the UK. Within it are numerous different reserves, and as the area makes up a single eco-unit, it is treated here as one location.

The Reserves and access areas:
Campfield Marsh and Bowness Reserve
South Solway Mosses, Bowness Common
Glasson Moss, Wedholme Flow and
Drumburgh Moss.
The special combination of habitats in
the Solway Peninsula makes up one
eco-system combining the intertidal
mudflats which surround it, together with
the wet pastureland and the peat-bogs of
the South Solway mosses. Different birds
respond in different ways. Some feed on
the rich pickings of the estuary mudflats,
and fly off inland, or roost on the edge of
the saltmarsh between tides, whereas
others spend the night on the sea and fly
inland to feed during daylight hours. If you
understand the system a little, you can
have a rich birdwatching experience.

Wildfowl and Waders Trail

This is one of the few places where birdwatching from your car is almost the sensible option. Alternatively, doing the trail by bike, or taking a day to walk it would be just as viable.

Start at the bridge over the Wampool (Grid ref: NY 228 576), where you might see waders such as Redshanks at low tide, and a variety of ducks. Turn left towards Anthorn. During the winter, for the next 1-2 miles, either side of the road, you have an excellent chance to see huge flocks of grazing Pinkfoot or Barnacle geese. The waterfront at Anthorn gives you access to the mudflats of the expanding Wampool, and the vast expanses of Moricambe Bay, with Skinburness and Grune Point in the distance. This is a nationally important site for all manner of ducks and waders.

As you continue around the peninsula, with the radio station on your right, keep an eye open for birds in the fields, especially at high tide. Large flocks of waders, especially Curlew, Oystercatcher and Lapwing are very common.

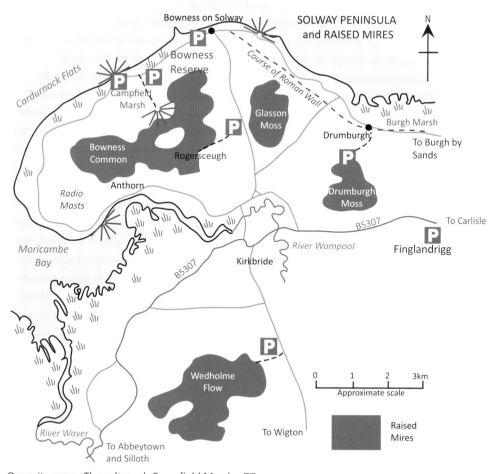

Opposite page: The salt-pool, Campfield Marsh   77

Wildfowl and Waders Trail (continued)

The layby at Campfield Marsh (Grid ref: NY180 609) gives you a fine view of the salt-marsh pool, together with the roosting areas for waders just above the normal high tide line. (For the rest of Campfield Marsh, see below.) There are other parking spots all the way towards Bowness, which can bring fine experiences of roosting birds.

Continue beyond Bowness to the parking places at little point overlooking the Eden Estuary. (Grid ref: 232 627) at the end of the strip owned by the National Trust. Here, especially either side of a high tide, you get fine views of waders.

Continue along the road towards Burgh by Sands, and you pass Burgh Marsh, part of the periodically-flooded salt marsh which forms part of the daily routine of ducks and geese every day, and waders with every tide.

Finish your drive by following the minor road which leaves Burgh village at the junction marked "Edward 1 Mon". Continue down the lane for about 1.5 miles until you reach the path beyond New Sandsfield (Grid ref: NY 343 614) which allows access to the tidal Eden, just before it widens out into the estuary proper. Here, depending on the tide you might see a wide range of geese, ducks and waders.

Campfield Marsh

Status: SSSI; and Nationally important RSPB Reserve.

Open all year; parking alongside road and at North Plain Farm. Wheelchair friendly to hide. Access is free, but donations are welcome.

How to get there

Grid ref: NY 202 616. Situated astride the minor coastal road between Bowness on Solway and Cardurnock. Accessed from the B5307 west of Carlisle or via Kirkbride. The saltmarsh and saltmarsh pools can be viewed from the road. From North Plain farm a good quality track leads inland for 800m to a hide, with good views over winter-flooded fields and the edge of Bowness Common.

Public Transport: Bus service 93 from Carlisle to Bowness; Service 71 from Carlisle to Kirkbride and Anthorn.

Campfield Marsh enjoys the whole range of the Solway Peninsula birdwatching habitats, and is equally enjoyable from the road or from the inland hide. Saltmarsh and pools along the road overlook the Eden Estuary, with its rich mudflats exposed at each low tide. Inland the reserve extends through wet and often flooded meadows to the edge of Bowness Common, England's biggest remaining lowland peatbog or "raised mire". Together these different environments present a wealth of birdwatching experience.

Birds to look out for

Birdwatching here varies both with the tides and with different seasons.
Look out for the high tide roost of thousands of wading birds along the edge of the salt marsh.
Winter: Enormous numbers of Pinkfoot and Barnacle geese; large numbers of Ducks, especially Teal and Wigeon; huge flocks of waders such as Oystercatcher, Redshank and Lapwing, "marching" up and down with the tides.
 Hen harriers are commonly seen from the hide, hunting along the edge of Bowness Common, together with other raptors such as Peregrine and Merlin, which prey on the massed ranks of small birds.
Spring: Breeding birds such as Lapwings and Curlew.
Summer: A time to enjoy the flowers and the range of small birds nesting all over the reserve. Listen out for the distinctive song of the Skylark.
Autumn: Look out for the return of the geese in September and October.
In spring and autumn there are many passage birds on their way to their breeding or overwintering grounds. Most famous are the three varieties of Skuas.

Redshanks at the water's edge

The Bowness on Solway Wildlife Reserve (Grid ref: NY 206 617) is adjacent to Campfield Marsh . It is managed by Cumbria Wildlife Trust and is based around an area of former gravel pits. Especially good in summer, with species such as Willow Tit, Willow Warbler and Black Cap.
Parking; Trails; Picnic spots.

Opp: Campfield Marsh near North Plain Farm

The Raised Mires

The Raised Mires
a) **South Solway Nature Reserve**
(Bowness Common, Glasson Moss and
Wedholme Flow).
Status: NNR; SSSI. Managed by English
Nature.
Parking; Marked trails; Information
boards; Free access all year. No other
facilities.
b) **Drumburgh Nature Reserve**
Status : NNR; SSSI; SAC. Managed by
Cumbria Wildlife Trust.
Parking; marked trails; free access; no
other facilities.

Curlew

The four Raised Mires are the last remaining examples of the sphagnum peat bogs which have formed here since the last ice age. Recent raising of the water-table and reversal of the drainage effected for peat extraction has resulted in the return of these places to their former wilderness habitat. They are important to birds, both for breeding and as high tide roosting places. For some species they are a specialist habitat.

Birds to look for

Bowness Common in winter is a reliable location for hunting Hen harriers. Also look out for Sparrowhawks.
Curlew and Snipe are regular breeders, and Black grouse are attracted to the diverse habitat of the edge of the mire. There is also a host of smaller breeding birds such as Meadow pipit and Stonechat. See Habitats and Species section, page 24.

Below: Secluded pond on the edge of Bowness Common

Above and below: Specialist peat bog flora

Grune Point & Moricambe Bay

Status: SSSI and part of an AONB. Not part of a formal reserve. Managed by the local farmer, with consultation from Natural England.
Parking is limited to roadside just before the cattle grid, and at the start of the track to Grune Point.
Grid ref (both): NY 128 558

How to get there

Grune Point is the peninsula running northeast from the village of Skinburness, accessible either on the coast road north from Silloth or from the "marsh road" which leaves the B5302 Silloth to Wigton road near Calvo.

Take the path which runs up the marsh side of the Grune, and return on the path which runs next to the sea on the north side. Good views over the marsh, especially of high tide roosting, also from the top of the sea dyke, which runs along the landward edge of Skinburness Marsh.

Public transport: Bus services 38 Wigton-Silloth-Skinburness and service 60 Maryport-Silloth-Skinburness.

Grune Point is a shingle spit with farmland bounded on the landward side by the mudflats of Moricambe Bay and the salt marshes of Skinburness and Calvo marshes, and on the west by the Solway Firth. It is not an official reserve but is one of North-West England's most spectacular birdwatching locations. Moricambe Bay is part of the internationally important Solway Coast, wintering ground for thousands of wildfowl and waders. The salt marshes are also an important high tide roost and feeding ground. Large bird numbers inevitably also attract raptors such as Peregrine falcons, Merlin, Buzzards and Sparrowhawks.

The combined habitats of intertidal mudflats, salt marsh, shingle beaches, sand dunes, hawthorn hedges, farmland and gorse produce a rich variety of nesting species, from Stonechats to Willow warblers, Wheatears and Song thrushes. Experience tells us that the best time for waders is 1-2 hours after high tide.

In general, although the Cumbria Coastal Way traverses Skinburness Marsh, be warned this is a dangerous place, and the our best advice is to keep off the marsh and to stick to the path around the Point.

Also keep to the paths, especially during spring and summer, so as not to disturb nesting species. Do not allow dogs to run free.

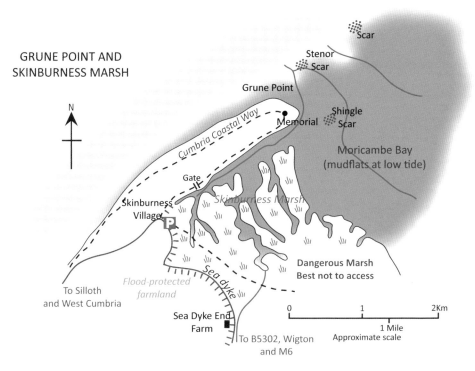

Some of my strongest chidhood memories are of the sounds of the birds, especially the unmistakable call of shelducks in the creeks during late summer and of skylarks and cuckoos along the path from Grune House to the Point.

Opposite: Skinburness Creek on Grune Point   83

Redshank

Shelduck

Birds to look for
All year round

Cormorant
Curlew
Greenfinch
Goldfinch
Grey heron
Greylag goose
Grey wagtail
Gulls (variety of species)
Lapwing
Linnet
Meadow pipit
Oystercatcher
Redstart
Reed bunting
Skylark
Snipe
Song thrush
Stonechat
Shelduck
Teal

Grey heron

Greylag goose

Passage Birds

(spring and autumn)
Large variety includes:
Little stint
Spotted redshank
Whimbrel
Common sandpiper
Green sandpiper
Curlew sandpiper

Ruff in winter plumage

Arctic tern

Summer Visitors

Grasshopper warbler
Lesser whitethroat
Ruff
Terns (Sandwich, Arctic,
Common and Little)
Whimbrel
Willow warbler
Wood sandpiper
Yellowhammer

Winter visitors

Barn owl	Merlin
Barnacle goose	Peregrine
Bar-tailed godwit	Pinkfoot goose
Dunlin	Pintail
Guillemot	Rock pipit
Goldeneye	Red-breasted merganser
Golden plover	Sanderling
Great-crested grebe	Scaup
Grey plover	Short-eared owl
Hen harrier	Snow bunting
Jack snipe	Turnstone
Knot	Twite
Kittiwake	Whooper swan
	Wigeon

Sanderling

Turnstone

Twite

Pintail

Goldeneye

Skylark

Grune Point in winter

Siddick Ponds

Status: Local Area Nature Reserve; SSSI
Grid ref: NY 001 309
Managed by Allerdale Borough Council
Open all year; no fee; cycle-way passes west side.
Parking at Board Mill or next to cycle way.
Facilities in Workington.

How to get there
Located on the north side of Workington next to the large Iggesund Board Mill and the A596 coast road from Maryport. Parking is in the board mill main car park. Alternatively, park next to Edgars' garage, nearer to Workington (Grid ref: NY 998 303), from where you can make access directly on to the cycle-way.

Public transport: Service X4 and X5 Keswick-Workington. Train from either Carnforth or from Carlisle.

This former quarry pit, created in the nineteenth century, is now an important wildlife refuge, with open water, extensive reedbeds and surrounding scrub and grassland. It is an easy-to-visit site, with lots going on, incorporating a range of habitats. The reserve is also very close to the sea, and so is attractive to a wide range of seabirds, wildfowl and waders depending on the seasons, the weather, and the different stages of the tide. In addition many of the 150+ recorded species choose to breed here.

Winter is the best time to see birds in numbers including Shovelers, Goldeneye, Tufted ducks, Pochard, Snipe, and the occasional Smew.

Reedbed Specialists

The reedbeds form the most important habitat at Siddick Ponds, so look for overwintering Bitterns and for nesting Reed warblers.

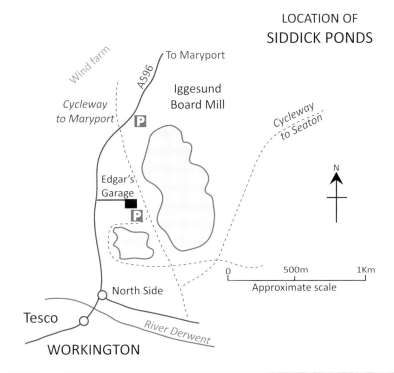

LOCATION OF
SIDDICK PONDS

Pochard

Tufted duck

Smew

Opposite: Wildlife and Industry side-by-side   87

St Bees Head

Status: RSPB Reserve
Parking at St Bees, Sandwith and Tarnflat Hall Farm
Open all year; free entry; donations welcome.
Best in Spring and Summer.
Grid ref: St Bees parking NX 960 119
Grid ref: North Head NX 940 145

How to get there

There are several possibilities depending on how far you wish to walk. Details are on the page opposite.

There are three safe viewing "platforms", safely fenced areas, all of which are south of the lighthouse.

The Coast to Coast Path passes through the reserve.

Public transport: Service 20, Whitehaven-Sandwith-St Bees. Train to St Bees and Whitehaven.

St Bees is the only large seabird nesting cliff in Cumbria and has the largest colony of nesting seabirds in the northwest of England. The red sandstone cliffs rise to about 100 metres and in an average season will have about 5000 nesting birds from April to July. Though there are large bird populations from early spring to mid-summer, during the rest of the year the cliffs are relatively deserted. The cliff walks provide a bracing and quiet walk, with few visitors, compared with the higher numbers at RSPB sites such as Leighton Moss, or even Campfield Marsh at times.

In spring the ungrazed cliffs are a mass of flowers, worth the walk alone.

From the top of the cliffs it is possible to see the Isle of Man, and a wide range of birds which tend to stay out to sea, especially Gannets.

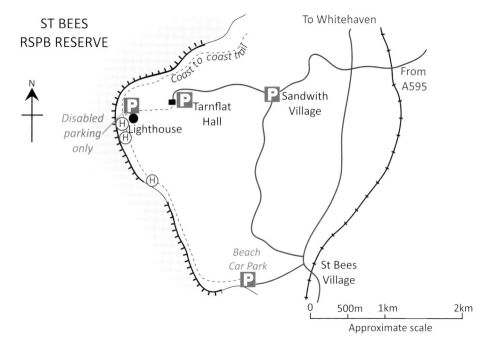

How to get there

The first two options are quite tough walking.

a) Park in St Bees (Grid ref: NX 960 118) and take the Coast to Coast trail along the cliffs to North Head (about 3 km, 2 miles).

b) Park in Whitehaven (Grid ref: NX 181 971) and take the Coast to Coast trail going south (about 4 km, 2.5 miles).

c) Park in Sandwith (Grid ref: NX 965 147) between Whitehaven and St Bees, and walk up the farm road to North Head.

d) Drive up the private road to Tarnflat Hall (Grid ref: NX 948 146) and park in the designated area north of the farm for a small charge. Those who find walking difficult can park next to the lighthouse, with permission.

Opposite: The lighthouse at St Bees Head   89

Birds to look for

There are nesting birds from April through to July. Breeding birds on the cliffs are likely to include Fulmars, Common guillemots, Black guillemots, Herring gulls, Jackdaws, Kestrels, Ravens, Little owls, Puffins, Razorbills, Peregrines, Rock pipits, Starlings, Stock doves and Wrens. Out at sea, look for various Terns, Gannets, Shearwaters and Skuas.

Razorbill

Herring gull nesting

Puffins

Guillemot community

St Bees Head

Opposite: It is worth the walk to see the wild flowers

91

Ravenglass, Eskmeals & Drigg

Eskmeals: SSSI and SAC. Managed by Cumbria Wildlife Trust. Open all year; no fee; parking and trails; no other facilities. No entry when the red flag is flying. Check firing range, tel: 012297 12200

Drigg Nature Reserve: SSSI and SAC. Owned and managed by Muncaster Estate. Parking; limited path system; permits no longer needed; facilities at Ravenglass.

Ravenglass Village waterfront is another good viewing spot. Park in the station at SD 086 965, and head left, down between the houses to view the estuary.

How to get there

For Eskmeals, Leave A595 at Waberthwaite. Continue just beyond the railway viaduct. Parking at Grid ref: SD 087 942. Road may be flooded at high tides. A path leads from the parking place to the sea and around the peninsula.

For Drigg, leave the A595 at Holmrook At Drigg village, turn left past the railway station and head towards the beach where parking is indicated at SD 048 985. A path leads south to the Irt estuary.
Public transport: Service 6 from Egremont . Service 14 from Millom.Train to Ravenglass. Miniature railway from Dalegarth, Eskdale.

At Ravenglass, the three rivers, Esk, Irt and Mite converge, with the dune systems of Eskmeals to the south and Drigg to the north. Until the1980s, Drigg had the biggest colony of nesting Black-headed gulls in Europe. The low-tide mudflats of the converging rivers provide a larder for a host of wildfowl and waders, and during rough weather, seabirds take shelter in the combined river mouths.

Add to your birdwatching experience with a visit to Muncaster Castle, which also has an Owl Centre, or a trip on the Ravenglass-Eskdale Railway.

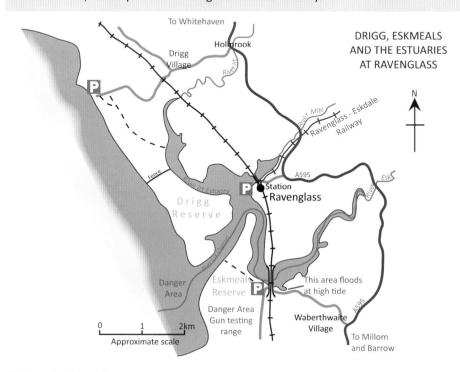

Birds to look out for

Ringed plover, Snipe, Dunlin, Curlew and Redshank are around all year, as are wildfowl such as Greylag geese, Shelducks and Red-breasted merganser. On the dunes there are always Skylarks.

In winter, Whooper swans, Goldeneye and Goosander will be amongst those birds arriving in the estuary, and the dunes will see Fieldfare and occasionally Twite.

Passage birds in spring and autumn might include Manx shearwaters, Common sandpiper, Black-tailed godwit, Whimbrel, various Skuas, together with Pinkfoot geese on their twice yearly migration.

Lots of birds guarantee the usual raptors. Look out for Peregrine, Buzzard, Barn owl and Little owl.

The enormous numbers of nesting Black-headed gulls, and also Terns, have gone. However, some gulls such as Lesser black-backed and Herring gulls do nest in the dunes, along with Eider duck.

Hodbarrow

Status: Hodbarrow RSPB Reserve.
Grid ref: SD 164 787 (best access point)
A flooded former iron ore mine, closed in 1967.
Free access, with unrestricted entry all year.
No facilities on site, but Millom is about a mile away.

How to get there
Approach only from the northwest via the caravan site at Haverigg. The "road" along the top of the sea wall is highly variable. You might prefer to walk the mile to the hide, near the lighthouse.

Grid ref: SD 175 780(lighthouse). Access to the car park at Hodbarrow Point really needs a 4 x 4.
Public transport: Service 511 Ulverston to Millom and Services M1 and M2 Millom to Haverigg.

Hodbarrow gives you a feast of birds and other wildlife throughout the year, especially the Great-crested grebe, nesting Sandwich and Little terns, the Red-breasted merganser, and the Sedge warbler, a summer visitor from Africa.

In winter there is a good range of wildfowl such as Wigeon and Pintail. From the access track, look seawards for waders such as Redshank, Golden plover and Oystercatchers, especially in the hours just after high tide. In spring and autumn this is also a good location for passage birds such as Curlew sandpiper, Little stint and Black-tailed godwit. Other wildlife includes over 270 species of plants, 19 species of butterfly and colonies of the rare Natterjack toad.

Hodbarrow Nesting Birds

Right in front of the hide, on the area called "the Island" you may find four out of the five nesting species of Tern occurring in Britain - Sandwich tern, Arctic tern, Common tern and Little tern, and also nesting Ringed plovers, Oystercatchers and Great black-backed gulls.

Other regular Hodbarrow nesters include:

Eider ducks, Great-crested grebes, Greylag geese, Herring gulls, Lapwings, Lesser back-backed gulls, Black-headed gulls, Red-breasted mergansers, and Tufted ducks.

A large annual moult of Red-breasted merganser occurs in late summer. In spring, look out for the amazing annual courtship displays of Great-crested grebes.

Arctic tern

Between the lagoons scrubland provides habitat for breeding birds, such as Warblers, Reed bunting, Whitethroat, Rock and Meadow pipit, Skylarks and Linnet.

Sandwich tern with young

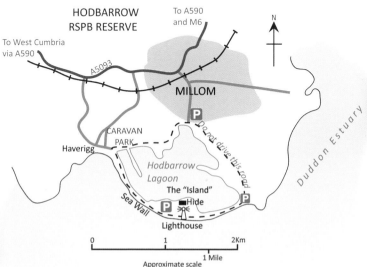

Great black-backed gull

Turnstone (winter)

Walney Island (South)

Status: SSSI; Wildlife Trust Reserve.
Managed by Cumbria Wildlife Trust.
Small admission charge; free to Trust members.
Resident warden; numerous marked trails and hides.
Some wheelchair access, though limited; toilets.
Best times to visit: April –August (Nesting gulls).
Autumn (Passage birds) Winter (Wildfowl and waders)

How to get there

Grid ref (Car Park): SD 216 620
From Barrow in Furness , head west across the bridge, following signs for "Walney Island". Over the bridge turn left. Soon, turn left on a minor road for Biggar, and continue south along this road for about 7 km (just over 4 miles), through the caravan site, until you arrive at the reserve, where parking is well-signposted. Then proceed along a variety of marked tracks and paths. Access may be restricted to certain areas during nesting.
Public transport only to Biggar Village, service 1 from Barrow.

As with many wildlife sites, South Walney is such a wild place, but still in view of modern industry and civilization, in this case Barrow. It is a habitat of sand-dunes, salt marsh, intertidal flats and lagoons, which are home to enormous numbers of breeding birds in spring and summer, and more waders and wildfowl in winter. Even the most casual birdwatcher cannot help but to be in awe of the 15,000 or more nesting Lesser black-backed and Herring gulls which seem to occupy every available space from April to the end of the summer.

Look for
Thousands of nesting Lesser black-backed and Herring gulls, a smaller number of Greater black-backed gulls nesting mainly around the lagoons, and UK's most southerly nesting eider ducks .

Lesser black-backed gull

In winter there are large numbers of seabirds, such as Red-throated divers, Red-necked and Slavonian grebes, Red-breasted merganser, Scaup, Long-tailed ducks, Goldeneye, Wigeon, and many more.

Herring gull

All year, and especially in winter, there are thousands of waders, including Turnstone, Ringed plover, Redshank, Greenshank, Dunlin, Curlew and Oyster-catcher.

Predators such as Peregrine, Hen harriers, and Merlin feasting on the huge amount of prey.

Great black-backed gull

In Spring and Autumn, Walney records enormous numbers of passage birds.

Pair of Eider ducks with young

Gull nest on the ground

Nesting gulls

UK has 40% of Europe's Lesser black-backed gulls, and a third of them nest at South Walney, sharing their colony with large numbers of Herring gulls. Some birds stay on the nesting ground all year, but most migrate further south for the first part of the winter. Male birds begin to establish territories early in the year, and by April there can be 15,000 to 20,000 pairs on the sand-dunes of South Walney. It seems that almost every available space is taken.

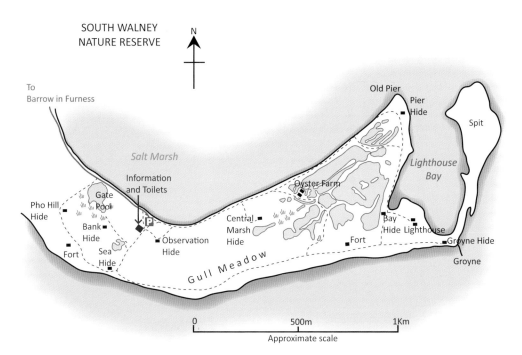

SOUTH WALNEY
NATURE RESERVE

N

To
Barrow in Furness

Old Pier

Pier
Hide

Spit

Salt Marsh

Lighthouse
Bay

Information
and Tolets

Oyster Farm

Pho Hill
Hide

Gate
Pool

P

Bank
Hide

Central
Marsh
Hide

Bay
Hide Lighthouse

Fort

Sea
Hide

Observation
Hide

Fort

Groyne Hide

Gull Meadow

Groyne

| 0 | | 500m | | 1Km |

Approximate scale

Eider Ducks

Eider ducks, the most prolific ducks in the world, only started nesting at South Walney, their most southerly nesting site, in UK, in 1949. Numbers of nests have fluctuated, with a maximum of about 1500 in the 1990s, and regularly between 200 to 300 today. Breeding success probably relates to the availability of food, in the Eider duck's case chiefly young mussels, supplies of which tends to fluctuate annually.

Nesting on South Walney starts in mid-April. The nest can be made from all sorts of material, but inside it is always lined with down from the duck's breast, one of nature's most amazing insulators. The Eider duck is a superb mother, hardly moving from the nest during incubation, with hatching occurring mid to late June. She is also extremely successful in defending her young from marauding Gulls, leading her ducklings down to water often under cover of darkness, usually to a communal crèche.

So well-camouflaged is the sitting mother, it is quite a challenge for you to identify nests, just above the high tide line. The males take no part in incubation or in rearing, and spend much of their time in "rafts" of several hundred on the sea. At South Walney they appear to favour the area around the old pier. Listen out for their distinctive "coo coo" call.

Male Eider duck   A group of Eider ducks

Passage Birds

Projecting into the Irish Sea at the end of a peninsula, Walney Island is probably the best place in northwest England to see passage birds, making their way either to their wintering or to their nesting grounds. Walney Island Observatory, started in 1963, has recorded over 250 different species, and the regular annual tally is about 180. The "Observatory" is a group of dedicated bird-watchers, rather than a particular place. Refer to *www.walneybo.blogspot.com*

Ruff in winter plumage

The autumn migration can be especially good.

A comprehensive list is superfluous, as it would contain hundreds of birds. However, an autumn visit might bring Manx and Sooty shearwaters, Storm and Leach's petrels, Arctic and Great skuas, Curlew sandpipers, and all the hirundanes, the Swallows, Swifts and Martins.

Walney Island (North)

Status: RIS; NNR; Managed by Natural England. No charge; free access all year. Parking at Grid ref: SD 170 699 Facilities in North Walney village.

How to get there
Cross the bridge from Barrow in Furness and turn right. After about 1 mile, at North Scale, turn left for North Walney village. There is a public car park at Earnse Point (where the buses turn) or you can take a rather bumpy but much used track, along the edge of the beach, for another half mile. The Nature Reserve is north of the airfield.

An alternative way is to park at North Scale, and take the path which leads around the eastern edge of the airfield towards the Walney Channel.

Public transport: Services 4/4A/4S to West Shore (Earnse Point)

North Walney is a large reserve of over 600 hectares. It takes in sand-dunes, dune slacks, salt-marsh heathland and mudflats, extending all the way to Sandscale Haws in the north, from where you can also view the northern end of the Channel. Though it probably suffers from lack of birdwatchers' attention because of the more accessible and perhaps spectacular South Walney, it is certainly worth a visit.

Birds to look for

There will always be large numbers of waders, especially Redshank, Ringed plover, Knot, Curlew, Dunlin and Oystercatcher. Also a good range of duck, especially Pintail and Shelduck. Also Red-breasted merganser.

Shelduck

Redshank

Ringed plover

Oystercatcher

Pintail

Opposite: North Walney west beach

Foulney Island

Status: SSSI; SAC; SPA; Cumbria Wildlfe Trust Reserve.
Grid Ref (car park): SD 233 656
Free access all year. Resident warden in breeding season.
Rough walking access; not wheelchair friendly; may be
cut off at highest tides.
Visitors should consult tide tables: www.tidetables.com

How to get there

From the Barrow in Furness to Ulverston coast road (A5087), follow the signs for Rampside and Roa island from the roundabout southeast of Barrow. About 400m along the Roa Island causeway, park in the small car park on the left.

Walk along to the left of a stone breakwater and then on to the sand and shingle ridge, which is Foulney Island. On the right are the mudflats between Foulney and Roa, Piel and Walney islands, and to the left, first salt marsh then the huge expanse of the mudflats of Morecambe Bay, with Humphrey Head , Morecambe and Heysham in the distance.

The walk to the point of the island is often fairly rough and is about 5.0 km (over 3 miles) round trip. There is no formal hide, but there is a small stone shelter, near the southern end, to give protection against westerly winds. Keep to the path, so as to avoid disturbing breeding birds.

Foulney Island is a delight. It is close to civilization but remote enough for nature to call all the shots.

Go there in spring and summer to see three of the species of terns, Arctic, Common and Little. Incredibly close to the path you will also see nesting Eider, Oystercatcher and Ringed plover, as well as unconcerned Skylarks and Meadow pipits. It is extremely helpful having a resident warden pointing out the nests which you passed within a metre or so on your walk out to the point.

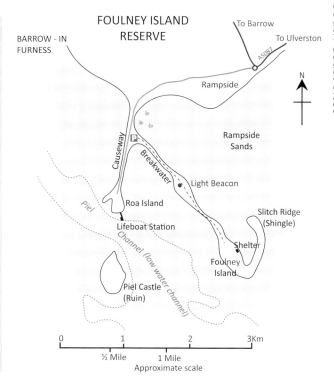

FOULNEY ISLAND RESERVE

To Barrow
To Ulverston
BARROW - IN FURNESS
A5087
Rampside
N
Causeway
Breakwater
Rampside Sands
Light Beacon
Piel
Roa Island
Slitch Ridge (Shingle)
Channel (low water channel)
Lifeboat Station
Shelter
Foulney Island
Piel Castle (Ruin)

0   1   2   3Km
½ Mile   1 Mile
Approximate scale

Little tern

Arctic tern

Sandwich terns

Well hidden Eider duck

Look especially for:
Nesting terns, Eider ducks, Ringed plovers, Skylarks and also Oystercatchers.

Black-tailed godwits

In Autumn and Winter the terns give way for the wildfowl and waders which come here in their thousands. See huge flocks of Knot, Oystercatcher, Godwit and Curlew advancing and retreating with each tide, as well as large numbers of wildfowl, including Brent geese, a wide range of Ducks, Great-crested grebes and Red-breasted merganser. On occasions, depending on the wind and tide there may be 2000 Eider ducks on the adjacent sea.

Morecambe Bay, Leven & Kent Estuaries

Status: EMS (European Maritime Site); SAC; SPA; Wetland of International Importance; SSSI; AONB. The most important estuary in Britain for seabird and wildfowl populations, with over 200,000 wintering wildfowl and 20,000 seabirds.

When to watch birds at Morecambe Bay
With the tide going out as far as 12km, birds are often far from land. So the best time is the hour before high water, when waders fly landward to roost, and a couple of hours after, as probing birds follow the falling tide.
Some sites are better on a medium tide, and others on a very high tide.

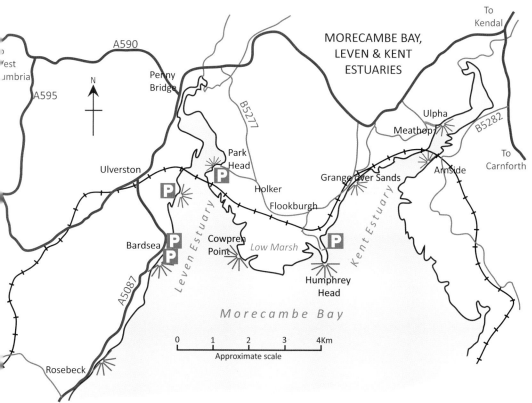

SOME LEVEN ESTUARY SITES

Bardsea-Wadhead Scar
Grid ref: SD303 744, on A5087 south of Ulverston .
Parking and Public Toilets.
Public transport: Service 11 Ulverston to Barrow. Train to Ulverston.
High tide wader roost on medium tides. Good Duck location.

Canal Foot-Ulverston
Grid ref: SD314 775. Approx 2km (1.5 miles) east of Ulverston. Coming south, turn left off A5087 immediately after railway bridge.
Public transport: Service X35 from Kendal. Train station at Ulverston.
Allows birdwatching in middle part of Leven estuary. Good for seabirds as the estuary narrows, especially with the channel close to shore.

Flookburgh Marshes
Cowpren Point.
Grid ref: SD 346 743. From Flookburgh walk 3km (2 miles) on right of way.
Public transport: Train to Flookburgh.

Park Head-Holker
Grid ref: SD 335 788. Take the B5278, about 1.5 km north of the village of Cark. Then turn left for about 2km (just over 1 mile), parking before the marsh. Access to estuary above the railway viaduct.
Large numbers of Black-headed and Common gulls. Good numbers of Shelduck, Teal, Mallard and Goldeneye.
Public transport: No convenient service, but Service X32 to within 2.5 km.

Humphrey Head lies between the Kent and Leven estuaries.
Grid ref SD: 394 734
Pubic transport: Train to Kent Bank.

Roost for waders at very high tides. The outmarsh has a reputation as a favoured location for the passage-birds such as Whimbrel.

Cumbria Coastal Way-Cark Airfield

Grid ref: SD 363 740. Head south from Flookburgh, and at West Plain farm walk west along the edge of the marsh on the Cumbria Coastal way.

One of the largest marshes. Best at very high tides, causing both waders and ducks up on to the saltmarsh. Reliable location for raptors such as Peregrine.

SOME KENT ESTUARY SITES

Grange Promenade (from railway station) towards Kent Bank

Grid ref: SD 412 782. Use A590 from M6 and follow signs for Grange over Sands. Public transport: Train to Grange over Sands.

Renowned location for watching waders feeding, and for Ducks, especially Shelduck and Pintail, Grebes and Divers.

Foulshaw Moss-Cumbria Coastal Way

Grid ref: SD 460 808. Leave the A590 at the Witherslack junction and head south for about 2km (just over 1 mile) on a minor road for Ulpha. Park where you meet signs for the Cumbria Coastal Way, and walk the remaining 1km to the seawall, giving a fine, elevated vantage point to view the upper estuary.

Foulshaw Marsh can be good for a range of birds. It often has a very large Gull roost; Geese, including Greylag and Pinkfoot use the mosses, and at high tide there is often a large roost of the normal range of waders.

Public transport: No convenient service.

Blackstone Point-Silverdale Marsh

Grid ref: SD 437 776. Park in Arnside at Grubbins Wood. Then walk 1.5 km (about 1 mile) to Blackstone Point. Continue on right of way to Far Arnside. Blackstone Point, just beyond the Cumbrian boundary gives close access to the Kent channel, with good numbers of Duck. The walk to Far Arnside allows views of Silverdale Marsh, with potential sightings of Shelduck, Wigeon and Pintail, as well as roosting waders.

Public transport: Train to Arnside from Carnforth.

Sunrise over Leven Estuary from Plumpton Marsh

Opposite: Humphrey Head from salt marsh

Leighton Moss

Status: RSPB Reserve, managed by the RSPB since 1964. Part of a larger SSSI between Warton Crag and Silverdale.
Grid ref (main car park): SD 480 752
Open 9am until dusk, shop and café 09.30- 17.00 (16.30 in winter). Wheelchair friendly paths and hides; parking; shop; toilets; café.
Entrance charges, with concessions and family ticket. Free to RSPB members. Contact 01524 701601.

How to get there

By road, leave the M6 at junction 35. Head for Carnforth and then take the minor road for Silverdale. After just under 5 km about 3 miles) the road crosses a railway, and after a further 800 metres (0.5 miles), Leighton Moss is signposted a short distance to your right.

Or take the road off the A6 at Yealand Redmayne, and follow the signs for Leighton Moss. This route passes reed beds on your left before arrival at the centre. Public transport: Service 552 from Kendal. Train to Silverdale. Silverdale railway station is only a minute's walk from the visitor centre.

With the largest reed-bed in northwest England and a unique range of birds, Leighton Moss is a delightful place to watch birds, both for the enthusiast and the beginner. It is highly accessible, has an excellent visitor centre, with good parking, a well-stocked shop, toilets, and a café selling home-baking.

The area was originally an inlet of Morecambe Bay and a peat moss. It was drained in the nineteenth century for agriculture but was allowed to re-flood in 1917 to become reedbed and fen.

It is home to a wide variety of birds, both in summer and winter, with a number of spectacular species. There is a wide range of wildfowl and waders, with some rather special and unusual birds (see below).

Around the main reedbeds, and also at the saltmarsh pools, there are comfortable hides. Some are close to the centre, whereas others require a walk of a few hundred metres.

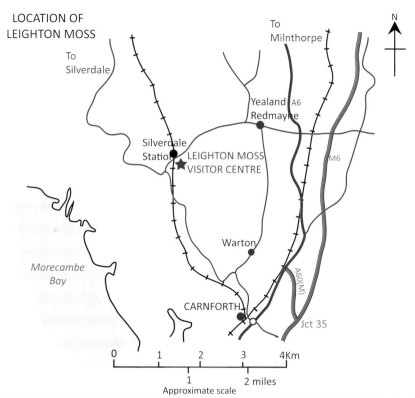

The Stars of the show

Avocets return for the spring and summer.

Bitterns here represent about 25% of the UK population.

Bearded tits are an attraction year round.

Marsh harriers are often to be seen hunting over the reed beds.

The shy Water rail is often to be seen in the channels along the edges of the reeds.

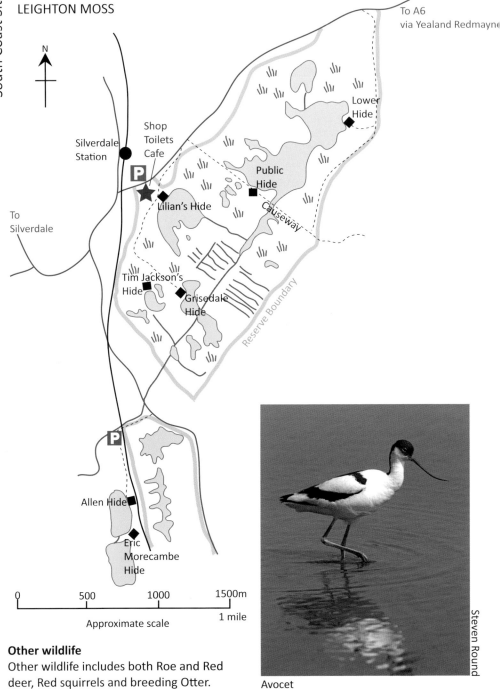

South Coast Sites

LEIGHTON MOSS

N

To A6
via Yealand Redmayne

Silverdale
Station

Shop
Toilets
Cafe

P

Lower
Hide

Public
Hide

Lilian's Hide

Causeway

To
Silverdale

Reserve Boundary

Tim Jackson's
Hide

Grisedale
Hide

P

Allen Hide

Eric
Morecambe
Hide

| 0 | 500 | 1000 | 1500m |

Approximate scale

1 mile

Steven Round

Avocet

Other wildlife
Other wildlife includes both Roe and Red
deer, Red squirrels and breeding Otter.

Some other locations, not covered in detail

Rockliffe Marsh
In spite of being a nationally important area for wildfowl, this book ignores Rockliffe Marsh because of lack of general easy access, together with use by wildfowlers. The marsh is of huge significance for waders and wildfowl, especially winter populations of Barnacle and Pinkfoot geese.

Longtown gravel pit
An important wintering spot for Swans and Geese, together with large numbers of waders such as Golden plover and Curlew. The reed beds are home to specialist species and also a stopping-off place for migratory Swifts and Swallows.

Silloth shore and docks
In spite of the big tidal range, along the promenade high and low water marks are close together, so that all sorts of avian delights occur within easy viewing. Look out for Great-crested grebes, Goldeneye and Red-breasted merganser, amongst many others. Expect a wide variety of waders, and seabirds such as Gannet and Red-throated diver not far off-shore.

Beckfoot to Dubmill Point
This coastal strip, between Silloth and Allonby, has much to recommend it, with a wide range of birds attracted to the numerous mussel-bed and the wide expanse of intertidal mud. Dubmill Point is also a rich passage-bird location.

Former gravel pit at Longtown

ACKNOWLEDGEMENTS

Most photographs in the book were taken by David and Rosemary Watson, except for the following:

David Feltham: Sedge warbler, page 39; Crossbill, page 61;
Little tern, page 101; Ringed plover, page 103
Brian Morrell, WWT Caerlaverock: Barnacle geese, page 72
Steven Round: Peregrine, page 47; Nuthatch, page 61;
Sparrowhawk, page 75; Avocet, page 110
George Sloan: Treecreeper, page 17

If you are interested in any of the photographs,
contact us on *watson.dr@btinternet.com*

Although every site was visited, some on numerous occasions, reference was also made to the following helpful publications.

Where to watch birds in Cumbria, Lancashire and Cheshire: Guest and Hutcheson
Birds of the Lake District: Mitchell
Bartholomew Birdwatching in the Lake District: Madders and Snow
Birdwatching Walks in the Lake District: Hindle and Wilson
Birdwatching in the Solway Coast: Brian Irving
The Lakeland Ospreys: David Ramshaw

If you are a beginner, one or more of the following books should be used in conjunction with this book:

RSPB Handbook of British Birds: Holden and Cleeves
RSPB Pocket Guide to British Birds: Harrap
RSPB Children's Guide to Bird Watching: Chandler and Unwin
Collins Bird Guide: Mullarey, Svesson, Zetterstrom and Grant
Collins Wild Guides: Birds: Holden

There are numerous useful websites, the best two of which are:
www.cumbriawildlifetrust.org.uk
www.cumbria-wildlife.org.uk